T0110700

Cambridge Elements ≡

Elements in Publishing and Book Culture
edited by
Samantha Rayner
University College London
Leah Tether
University of Bristol

DIVERSITY AND INCLUSION IN YOUNG ADULT PUBLISHING, 1960–1980

Karen Sands O'Connor
Newcastle University

CAMBRIDGE
UNIVERSITY PRESS

CAMBRIDGE
UNIVERSITY PRESS

Shaftesbury Road, Cambridge CB2 8EA, United Kingdom

One Liberty Plaza, 20th Floor, New York, NY 10006, USA

477 Williamstown Road, Port Melbourne, VIC 3207, Australia

314–321, 3rd Floor, Plot 3, Splendor Forum, Jasola District Centre,
New Delhi – 110025, India

103 Penang Road, #05–06/07, Visioncrest Commercial, Singapore 238467

Cambridge University Press is part of Cambridge University Press & Assessment,
a department of the University of Cambridge.

We share the University's mission to contribute to society through the pursuit of
education, learning and research at the highest international levels of excellence.

www.cambridge.org
Information on this title: www.cambridge.org/9781108827836

DOI: 10.1017/9781108900584

First published 2022

A catalogue record for this publication is available from the British Library.

ISBN 978-1-108-82783-6 Paperback
ISSN 2514-8524 (online)
ISSN 2514-8516 (print)

Diversity and Inclusion in Young Adult Publishing, 1960–1980

Elements in Publishing and Book Culture

DOI: 10.1017/9781108900584

First published online: October 2022

Karen Sands-O'Connor

Newcastle University

Author for correspondence: Karen Sands-O'Connor,
Karen.Sands-O'Connor@newcastle.ac.uk

ABSTRACT: This Element examines the early years of British young adult (YA) publishing at three strategic publishing houses: Penguin, Heinemann, and Macmillan. Specifically, it discusses their YA imprints (Penguin Peacocks, Heinemann New Windmills, and Macmillan Topliners), all created at a time when the population of Britain was changing and becoming more diverse. Migration of colonial and former colonial subjects from the Caribbean, India, and Africa contributed to a change in the ethnic makeup of Britain, especially in major urban centres such as London, Birmingham, and Manchester. While publishing has typically been seen as slow to respond to societal changes in children's literature, all three of these YA imprints attempted to address and include Black British and British Asian readers and characters in their books; ultimately, however, their focus remained on white readers' concerns.

KEYWORDS: Black British, young adult, British Asian, publishing, literature

ISBNs: 9781108827836 (PB), 9781108900584 (OC)
ISSNs: 2514-8524 (online), 2514-8516 (print)

Contents

Introduction: Citizens of Tomorrow, Reading Today: Catering to the New 'Teenager' Reader in Britain

We set out to present the new department in a 'with-it' way . . . We tried to provide books which would to some extent give the teenagers an insight into life outside their own sphere. *(Knight 145)*

'The important thing,' as [Sivanandan] later recalled, was to encourage people to read – 'these were not kids who would read.' *(Waters 59)*

Although the word appeared in the British lexicon much earlier, 'teenagers' began getting serious attention – in the media, from the government, and as consumers – following World War II. Major changes in British society, including the extension of compulsory education and increasing availability of spending money for young people, meant that teenagers became a matter of concern. Adults worried that the new generation would not be 'properly' educated to make the most of their newfound consumer ability. An article in the *Manchester Guardian* in 1961, 'What Teenagers Buy', suggests that 'the social consequences' of teen spending 'cannot be ignored' (12); the anonymous author points to teenage reading of pulp magazines among the working classes and wonders 'what sort of education is it that lets the children of one class go into the world prepared to have their needs, real or fictitious, satisfied (or left unsatisfied) with rubbish?' (12). Getting teenagers of all classes to spend free income on the 'right' reading might make or break the nation.

But who *were* teenagers? What *was* the right reading for them? And how could adults encourage teenagers to choose these books? Prior to 1950, the answer had largely been to give British middle- and upper-class readers higher-vocabulary children's classics and adult classics that would maintain moral standards. These included, according to Stuart Hannabuss, books that developed nationalism and were morally 'respectable' (128) such as Charles Kingsley's *Westward Ho!*, Harriet Beecher Stowe's *Uncle Tom's Cabin*, and Victor Hugo's *Les Misérables*, all of which Hannabuss suggested were being recommended into the 1940s. But the British population was changing throughout the 1950s and 1960s, as people from the former colonial Empire, particularly Caribbean and South Asian migrants, began to make Britain their home and working-class children were required to stay in school longer. These teenagers had been almost entirely left out of the conversation, deemed by many (if they acknowledged them at all) as populations that 'didn't read'. As the 1950s went on, a broader consideration of the whole teenage population became a more frequent part of the national conversation; nonetheless, it continued to be a conversation dominated by white middle-class adult voices trying to solve the 'problem' of these readers, particularly in the book world.

'Tomorrow, for Better or Worse, They Will Be Britain': Reading the Teenager

In the 1950s, British teenagers began to capture the public's attention – and generally not in a good way. A *Picture Post* article from March 1957 that tried to establish 'the truth about teenagers' argued: 'Today they are the young people who suck sticky brown stuff through straws, stay out too late, wear the wrong clothes, and think they know it all. But to-morrow, for better or worse, they will be Britain' (Philpott 11). Articles in the *Daily Mail* worried about idle teens turning to gang warfare against the police ('Gang Attacks Police' 7; 'Teenage Danger' 5), rock and roll (Iddon 6), and bad habits imported from America (Pocock 4). In fact, the *Daily Mail* was so critical of teenagers throughout the late 1950s that it prompted teenager David Martin to respond, 'For how much longer must Britain's four million teenagers be generalised as "that lot of nuisances"' (6). Articles blaming lack of religion ('Church Urges Need for Sex Education' 5), bad parenting (J. Hall 2), and education ('Hard for Youth to Grow Up' 5) for teenager delinquency were common throughout the media, pinning responsibility on adults for the perceived decline in teenage behaviour. Whatever the cause, the media saw teenagers as a problem that had to be solved by the British public – and more specifically, by adults.

At the same time, teenagers were also being acknowledged as a powerful economic force. Following the release of a 1958 Earnings Census from the Ministry of Labour, which suggested that teenage disposable income in the country amounted to 900 million pounds, a *Sunday Times* reporter labelled teenagers as 'an increasingly important and idiosyncratic market' ('Big "Teenage" Spending' 8). Teens spent about half their money on clothing, alcohol and tobacco, and sweets, but Mark Abrams pointed out that 'a good share of the balance goes on entertainment goods – "pop" records, gramophones, romantic magazines and fiction paperbacks, visits to the cinema and dance hall' (6). Out of this list of teenage purchases, it is teenage reading that is easiest for adults to target and control, as a good deal of the pop music and cinema came from America (or, in certain areas, the Caribbean, with ska and calypso being popular). Reading also could impart moral messages in ways that music and cinema could or did not, and this gave adults a sense that they were also tackling the perceived moral decline of teenagers.

Reading also had the benefit of being done in school – and education for young people had been extended, with the school leaving age raised to 15 in 1947 (it would be raised again to 16 in 1972). As Derek Gillard explains in *Education in England*, the 1944 education act, written as the horrors of war and fascism were coming to light, required schools to contribute to both spiritual and moral education of future citizens. Teenagers would be in school longer, and their moral instruction would therefore be in the hands of the education system for longer as well. But as I. G. K. Fenwick notes in *The Comprehensive School 1944–1970*, by 1948, 'secondary school had to cope with nearly 400,000 more pupils remaining in full-time education' (39). Teachers had to find a way to keep these students interested while teaching them values in what were often overcrowded classrooms filled with students who did not want to be there.

Not only schools, but libraries were changing too. Surveys done by librarians in the late 1950s and early 1960s found that library use by teenagers was low. Some suggested that teens were visiting 'what might be called pornographic bookshops' instead of public libraries; almost all librarians lamented that teenagers were more interested in 'jazz' (Tomlinson 100) or 'pop music' (Knight 145) than reading. Libraries such as the newly created Teenage Library in Lincoln piped pop music into reading rooms, but having a place where teenagers could come to 'listen to records, dance and have coffee' (Knight 146) did not solve the problem of getting teens to read. After all, teens could do (and most did) all these things at community centres and youth clubs. Books had to appeal to teenagers in presentation as well as content; Aidan

Chambers noted in 1969 that '60 per cent of the population rarely, if ever, enter a library for any reason at all, let alone to borrow from the banks of plastic-covered novels lining the fiction shelves' (*Reluctant Reader* 17). Margaret Marshall, in *Libraries and Literature for Teenagers* (1975), agreed; in one experiment she offered a variety of titles to teenagers, and found that 'never at any time did those teenagers, aged fourteen to twenty, even touch any of the hardbacks on the table' (252), preferring paperbacks and comics. And if 'What Teenagers Buy' (1961) was to be believed, books would have to be found alongside magazines; new, cheaper formats suitable to newsagents would be more likely to draw in those turned off by school reading.

People Like Us: The British Teenager, Reading

Above all, research suggested that most teenage readers – though they might pick up the occasional historical novel or science fiction – wanted 'books about people like us' (Trotman 72). By the mid-1960s, some publishers were listening to their potential teenage readers; Naomi Lewis, in *The Best Children's Books of 1964*, noted that realistic fiction 'holds most of the clues to changes in taste, technique or theme. There are, for instance, several attempts to write for the over-fourteens in, more or less, their own terms' (9). Nonetheless, there was, in the aftermath of World War II, a lack of contemporary realist fiction based on teenage protagonists in Britain, and this was a gap that publishers of young adult (YA) literature (or teenage fiction, as it was called early on) would seek to fill throughout the 1960s and 1970s, with publishers creating imprints especially for them.

The novels about 'people like us' that teenagers wanted were often imported from America in the years following World War II. By the early 1950s, American youth had *bildungsroman* from both the northern and southern parts of the country, featuring both boy and girl protagonists. Betty Smith's *A Tree Grows in Brooklyn* (1943), Carson McCullers' *A Member of the Wedding* (1946), and J. D. Salinger's *Catcher in the Rye* (1951) all highlighted the unique confusion and small joys of adolescence and its centrality to American identity. All had features of the YA novel that would become standard to the genre: frank discussion of sex, vivid and often slangy language, and an uncertainty surrounding traditional morality. *Catcher in the Rye* also featured a first-person narration that, like the previous century's *Adventures of Huckleberry Finn* (Twain 1884) gave an immediacy and focus that frequently characterise YA literature. Although Britain did produce novels with some of these characteristics, they were either – as in the case of the novels of Jean Rhys, such as *Voyage in the Dark* (1934) – shelved firmly in the adult section, or – in novels such as Dodie Smith's *I Capture the Castle* (1948) – acceptable because they were reasonably chaste and within the bounds of socially acceptable morality. And while many American teenagers could relate directly to characters like Holden Caulfield, Frankie Addams, or Francie Nolan, British teen readers would rarely have had the experience of being forced by poverty into being a call girl (*Voyage's* Anna Morgan) or trying to gain the attention of a wealthy suitor in order to save the family castle (*Capture's* Cassandra Mortmain).

In fact, the novels of Rhys and Smith highlight two particularities of British novels about teenagers that made them different from American novels. First, class played a large role in British novels for young people, who were mostly given middle- or upper-class protagonists in their books (even if these characters were temporarily, as Cassandra Mortmain, suffering genteel poverty). Second, colonialism haunted the British novel. Anna Morgan, in Rhys' novel, is white but from the Caribbean; she speaks like the Afro-Caribbean servants who surrounded her in childhood, and she is misunderstood, used, and eventually rejected by the British (particularly men). Whereas Francie Nolan, part of an Irish-American immigrant family, experiences many of the same things as West Indian immigrant to Britain Anna Morgan, *A Tree Grows in Brooklyn* quickly became classic reading for American teenagers both in and out of schools, while *Voyage in the Dark* has never been a recommended text for British teenage readers.

The rise of the British teenage novel coincided with and was affected by the demise of British colonialism and subsequent migration of thousands of colonial and former colonial subjects to 'the Mother Country' from the late 1940s to the late 1960s. People from the Caribbean, South Asia, and Africa began coming to Britain to fill post-war labour shortages and escape the economic and political effects of Britain's colonial rule following

World War II. By the time that publishers began creating specific 'teenage' imprints in Britain, teenage readers (and potential consumers) were no longer exclusively white or middle-class. Increasingly, people of colour that appeared as servants, foreigners, and villains in white British children's books were now white readers' neighbours. While white British adults might avoid coming into regular contact with 'New Commonwealth Immigrants', their children interacted with teens of colour in school, and through the medium of popular music in multiracial clubs and community centres. Many white teenagers were intrigued by the lives of their Black and Asian British counterparts. Black and Asian British teenagers wanted to read about 'people like us' just as much as white British readers did. But many publishers, librarians, and teachers did not give them the opportunity. In fact, books published for teenagers in the 1960s and early 1970s often reflected the notion that 'new immigrants' were one of the many problems that had to be confronted and solved by white British teens. In this way, the publishing world mirrored the wider culture. As Paul Gilroy wrote, 'the black presence in post-war Britain has been constantly identified as a source of problems' for white Britain to fix (89).

All-Consuming Britishness: Creating Literature for the British Teenager

Much research has yet to be done on the history of early British YA, and an Element such as this one cannot cover the subject completely. I intend to examine this history, therefore, through the lens of what the changing British teen population was offered by three early YA imprints in Britain: Penguin Peacock, Heinemann New Windmill, and Macmillan Topliners. These imprints all took different approaches, both to their intended readers and to multiracial Britain. The editors of these series, Kaye Webb (Peacock), Ian Serraillier (New Windmill), and Aidan Chambers (Topliners), all had clear and distinct values and goals for books they published, but these goals differed considerably. Webb and Chambers published for different audiences, but both utilised paperbacks to appeal to their readership. New Windmill books, in contrast, were sold exclusively to schools and school libraries, but under Serraillier's editorship responded to changes in British society in ways more similar to mainstream than educational publishers.

Of the three imprints, only New Windmill is still active, largely due to its educational market. However, in this book I will focus only on the early period of Serraillier's editorship. Editors had enormous autonomy during this period, especially children's book editors who often worked alone or with only a small staff. Thus a single person had power to influence the reading choices that teens were offered. The years between 1960 and 1980 were formative to both British YA literature and to attitudes about race and diversity within Britain. As librarians, teachers, and booksellers across Britain struggled to define good literature for teenagers and debated ways to get that literature to targeted audiences, Black and Asian Britons faced housing, educational, and employment discrimination; fought police oppression and Margaret Thatcher's sus laws; and attempted to introduce a literature of their own to British society. Teenage literature of this period demonstrates the crossover between society's values and literature it deemed valuable for its youth. I am particularly interested in how these publishing imprints introduced authors and characters of colour to their series, their attitudes towards Britishness and colonialism, and their depiction of a 'universal' teen experience to understand ways that British society as a whole defined itself. Often, attitudes of editors towards inclusion of Black and Asian British characters in YA literature shaped the genre, and perhaps also their audience, long beyond the shelf life of the books.

Literature for British children has long been a space for and about middle-class white readers and characters, and attempts to make that space more inclusive have frequently been met with arguments about 'literary quality'. The highest award given to British literature, the Carnegie medal, has often defended itself against critics with this argument; as Pearson and colleagues comment in 'Prize Culture and Diversity in British Children's Literature', 'criticisms of [the Carnegie's] failure to honour books that reflected the diversity of British society or that appealed to a wide range of child readers were frequently met with an emphasis on the Medal's mission to award literary quality' (100). But this argument about quality suggests particular criteria. Emphasis in children's literature has been on elements such as plot, theme, and characterisation to determine literary quality, valued according to a white European standard. Books that do not meet this standard are often dismissed as 'political' and therefore not literary, but Donnarae MacCann, in *White Supremacy in Children's Literature* (1997), argues that 'the cultural specificity of a work is not its political content alone; it is also part of its stylistic content' (xxi). Literature written by and about white British people is not apolitical, but literature written by and about Black and Asian Britons is not unliterary either.

This same argument about quality, however, can also be applied to YA literature. Historically, gatekeepers of YA literature – as I will demonstrate in this Element – worried more about literary quality than actual teenage opinion, whether they were publishing for mainstream or educational markets. Some editors, like Kaye Webb, clung to the idea of giving teenagers 'proper' literature, with elevated language and a quality of 'timelessness' such as was found in award-winning children's books or adult classics. Others, like Aidan Chambers, offered young adults books attempting to provide relevant and up-to-the-minute language, style, and plots. Both approaches make claims about, but also attempt to define, what a teenager is and should want to be and read. In either case, the defining characteristic of young adult readers, according to editors, is that they still had to be shaped and defined by a book industry made up of adults. Margaret Marshall argues that 'many British and American teachers and librarians see reading also as a tool by which civic sense and democracy can be shaped' (41). Marshall might have added YA book editors to this group; although Webb and Chambers were at opposite ends of the spectrum, they and Serraillier all felt it necessary to teach teenagers how to become part of British society. While there is some evidence that these editors engaged with young people at the beginning of the process (to see what kinds of books they liked or were reading), there was no concerted effort to find out what teenagers thought of the books that the imprints actually published. This is one reason that actual teenage response to literature is minimal in this book. The archives of Webb, Chambers, and Serraillier do not include many examples of letters from teenagers (Chambers' archive includes the most, but these do not concern titles mentioned in this Element), nor did they tend to use teenage reviews in their advertising. All three editors, however, responded to other white British adults – parents, teachers, and librarians – about whether or not books they published were good for teenagers.

These editors' engagement with Britishness and emphasis on language and meaningful experience had particular, even exceptional, consequences for teenage readers of colour. For most of the period I am considering, Black and Asian Britons were labelled 'New Commonwealth immigrants' even if they were born in Britain. They were *in* Britain, and sometimes even *of* Britain, but they were rarely seen as British. Philip Cohen comments that during this period, white Britons claimed that 'Black separatism is intrinsically racist *and* that there is nothing racist about a 'British' way of life in which little or nothing of Black culture is officially recognised' (25). Books for teens may have included Black or Asian characters, but the focus was on 'British' – that is to say, white – characters. At a time when Black and Asian British young people were experiencing discrimination in education, employment, and policing, literature written about them by white authors rarely addressed any of their concerns. Novels from all three of the imprints I discuss include characters of colour, but these characters are rarely described as British. Characters of non-European heritage are often only encountered outside of Britain in these books. Even when Black and Asian characters are present, books often focus on white British concerns about them. YA novels of this period define who belongs to Britain as well as who belongs in books – and in most cases, this results in literary apartheid.

1 A Whole Raft of Readers Unaddressed: Peacocks, the 'Reading Teen', and Racial Diversity

In contrast with librarians wondering whether to buy record players to entice teenagers to come in and – maybe – pick up a book, Kaye Webb began the Peacock imprint of Penguin in 1962 because readers of Puffins wanted more to read. Felicity Trotman in 'Remembering Peacock' comments, 'So many young people said "I'm too old for Puffins – what do I read now?" that it was very clear there was a whole raft of readers whose needs weren't being addressed' (71–2). Webb, like other early publishers of YA literature, had to fight to get company executives to see the need for a new imprint; bookstores had no room for separate teenage sections and publishers themselves did not see financial reward in expanding children's lists in this way. But Webb held her ground and, thanks in no small part to the success of Puffin, she was allowed to devote part of her book quota to her new venture. She would remain editor, and continue publishing Peacocks, until 1979, although from 1977, she left most of the decision-making about Peacock titles to her sub-editors, Dorothy Wood and Tony Lacey.

Unlike many editors today, Webb had a strong measure of control over every aspect of Peacock, from choice of book to choice of cover. Steve Hare notes that 'Kaye Webb's assistant Doreen Scott had her kitchen requisitioned for the cover photograph' (294–5) of *The Peacock Cookery Book*, and Webb instructed the author to make a dish from the book to place in the kitchen. This kind of editorial control, only possible with a small list directed at a particular audience, shaped the Peacock brand, especially in the early years. Webb's particular vision of Peacock readers, teens who always already liked reading, meant that Peacock books were designed to appeal to the same demographic as Puffin readers – 'articulate, literate and imaginative children from book-lined homes', as Valerie Grove put it (66). In 1962, that demographic in Britain was almost exclusively envisioned as white and middle-class. Black and Asian British youth, often socio-economically disadvantaged and placed into Educationally Sub Normal (ESN) classrooms at a significantly higher rate than white children (see Coard), were not seen by white adults as readers.

Additionally, Webb's success with Puffin meant that she did not have to try to court Black and Asian British readers. In the 1960s age of advertising, Webb knew how to secure brand loyalty from her readership, and Puffin readers would eventually become Peacock readers. While loyalty among Puffin, Peacock, and Penguin readers continue to make the company the most historicised publisher in Britain (it is the only publisher with a collector's society, its own journal, and a postgraduate bursary devoted to its history), Webb's branding of Peacock as a white middle-class imprint meant not only that readers of colour largely felt excluded but white teen readers received a distinctly skewed view of diversity from Peacock books.

Spreading the Peacock's Plumes: Expanding the Children's Department

Kaye Webb took over from Eleanor Graham as chief editor of Penguin's children's division, Puffin, in 1961, but she was keen to put her mark on the company. Puffin children's books appeared during World War II when Penguin editor Allan Lane decided to capitalise on a population of children who had suffered under wartime restrictions, many bombed out, far from home, unable to access public libraries. Like Penguin, Puffin was designed as a paperback-only imprint so that books could be produced cheaply. Puffin story books first appeared in 1941 under Graham's editorship. She remained editor of Puffin until 1961, and her work set the tone for the brand.

As a paperback imprint, Puffin was a mix of reprints of books published in hardback by other companies and a few original titles. Graham commented that she conceived of Puffins as 'definitely not a series of out-of-copyright classics. What we wanted was the best of the *new* classics of the new generation' (117). At first, she faced considerable resistance from traditional children's publishers, booksellers, and libraries. However, Kate Wright suggests that 'Graham, admirably, was not prepared to compromise over quality. She published what she could, provided that it met her high standards' (43). Her focus on quality meant that she only published around twelve new titles a year. When Webb inherited Puffins from Graham, the list was relatively small compared to many children's publishers, but it had established itself as an imprint providing inexpensive editions of stories for the reading child.

Kaye Webb's own sensibilities were in sympathy with Graham's in terms of avoiding popular, flash-in-the-pan bestsellers in favour of 'new classics', but she felt that Puffin could do much more than it had been doing. Webb's ideas included expanding the list by periodising childhood reading. Her editorial notes, now archived at Seven Stories, the United Kingdom's National Centre for Children's Books, include a 1961 plan to place Puffins into four categories: junior Puffins for readers up to the age of eight, Puffins for eight- to eleven-year-olds, Puffin Seniors for those between eleven and thirteen or fourteen, and Peacocks, for fourteen- to sixteen-year-olds ('Tony Godwin: Summary of Conversation' f2). Webb was most concerned to get Peacock right; she wrote, 'The first batch of Peacocks approximately eight titles should include as large a number of specially commissioned books as possible. To make strongest possible impact' ('Tony Godwin' f2; grammar in original). However, this was not a simple prospect. Little had been written specifically for British teenagers in 1962, and Allan Lane gently suggested to Webb that she use 'existing books and or existing penguins might do two editions with diff covers' ('Kaye Webb Puffin Notes in Diary Form' f4; grammar in original). The first three years of Peacock included just two specially commissioned books, both non-fiction, both from 1964: Rex Hazlewood and John Thurman's *The Peacock Camping Book* and Betty Falk's *The Peacock Cookery Book*.

In terms of fiction from these early years, Felicity Trotman notes that Peacocks were generally books 'originally published for adults but [which] had engaging and appropriately youthful characters or the sort of adventure a young reader could really identify with' (72). Only one, Marjorie Bowen's *The Viper of Milan* (1964), had been written by a teenager, and one other had been written *for* teenagers, but in America: Beverley Cleary's *Fifteen* (1962). In fact, there was little that could be called contemporary British fiction on the list; most was either historical or set outside Britain (with rare exceptions, such as Dodie Smith's *I Capture the Castle*, set in Britain's recent past).

Outside, Over There: Early Peacocks, the British Empire, and Diversity

Peacocks published before 1971 represented Kaye Webb's idea of what (white) teenagers wanted and should be given to read. Felicity Trotman suggests that Webb tried to 'find a range of titles. Most readers have preferences: they enjoy historical novels, or animal stories, or science fiction, or adventures, or fantasy – to publish for older children meant trying to find books in every category' (72). Because Peacock was designed as an upwards extension of the children's imprint Puffin (rather than downwards from the adult Penguin), Webb's early choices tended to avoid sexuality and language that might offend parents (including both swearing and slang). Parents of Peacock readers were much more likely than other parents to read their teenager's literary choices and complain loudly about them to Webb if they found them inappropriate. Webb, through Peacocks, acted *in loco parentis* for teenage reading. It is perhaps unsurprising then that as Webb scanned adult lists for suitable titles, she tended to settle on older books, where sexuality was presented subtly and language more regulated.

However, Webb's concern about language did not extend to racist language and ideas, which were rife in 1960s Peacocks. Often these older 'classic' books were written from a British imperial perspective. This is not surprising; it was not until the year that Kaye Webb took over Puffin that British colonies Jamaica and Trinidad gained their independence, and most Peacocks published during Webb's first three years as editor were originally written long before independence for most Asian and African colonies. And while Empire-era literature was often seen as moral, because it instilled a sense of duty and loyalty to country, John MacKenzie argues that it also promotes a 'sense of national and racial superiority' (224) for presumed-white readers. Sheila Patterson notes that in 1963, Black and Asian youth were seen by many white Britons in terms of what they learned from 'the colour-class myths of an outmoded colonial past' (350) and that books painted Black and Asian people as 'primitive, pagan, and sexually unin-hibited' (350).

While there is evidence, discussed later in this chapter that parents objected to books that hinted at cross-racial romantic relationships, racist language apparently did not bother white parents – or Webb herself.

Many 1960s Peacocks were aimed at boys, which Trotman said was a deliberate choice on Webb's part because 'girls will read about almost anything, whereas boys won't' (72). In fact, in the back of Peacocks until at least 1970, further reading suggestions were listed under two categories,

'General' and 'Especially for Girls'; the General section, presumably designed more 'especially for boys' than girls, was always a longer list. But it was in the boys' adventure story that racial stereotyping tended to be at its strongest. This is partly because white boy characters were more likely to be placed in situations outside England where they came into contact with people from other cultures. The boys' adventure story rests on the white boy character's success in domination of land and people, and his inherent right to do so. It was a tradition that continued well into the twentieth century (as did the British Empire), and can be found in early Peacocks in novels by Crosbie Garstin and John Buchan.

Garstin's *The Owls' House* was first published in 1923 by Heinemann; a Penguin edition appeared on adult lists in 1936, and Webb published it as a Peacock in 1964. This publishing history is perhaps part of why white parents did not object to the novel's excessive sexism and racism; they may well have read the book themselves in the distant past, and either not cared about or not remembered racist passages or demeaning discussions of women, though it is harder to explain why Webb – who presumably read books before choosing them for Peacock – had no problem with it. Garstin's white British hero, John Penhale, marries an outsider in British society, a 'gypsy girl'. Yet one of their sons, Ortho, lumps people of different races and religions together as part of the same, animal-like group. When Ortho gets shipwrecked and then rescued by another ship, it has a crew of 'such men! Brown, yellow, white, and black, with and without beards. . . . They paid no attention to him whatever, but chatted and spat and laughed, their teeth gleaming white in their dark faces, for all the world like a tribe of squatting baboons' (183). It continues: 'At his first roar every black and brown ape on deck pulled his hood up and went down on his forehead, jabbering incoherently. They seemed to be making some sort of prayer towards the East' (183). One Black person is depicted as 'a giant Negro' with 'a severed head' attached to his belt (222); another is called 'a Sambo' (251). None of this seems appropriate for young readers in Britain, which, by the 1960s, had nearly a million citizens with African, Afro-Caribbean, or Asian origins (Rose 99).

Overt racism such as that in Garstin's book is problematic, but the more subtle (and it is a matter of degrees – most of what I discuss here would hardly be considered subtle now) and casual racism found in works by authors such as John Buchan also fed into a sense of white British superiority. Buchan was best known for *The Thirty-Nine Steps* (1915), for which Penguin had acquired paperback rights in the 1950s along with his other novels about his 'everyman' hero, Richard Hannay. Webb published two of these novels as Peacocks; the fourth book in the sequence, *The Three Hostages* (orig. 1924; Peacock 1963), and the second, *Greenmantle* (orig. 1916, Peacock 1964). The novels are fast-paced and exciting, and filled with casual and direct racism. White British people (particularly men) wander the world with impunity, easily dominating land and 'natives'. In the opening of *The Three Hostages*, for example, readers are introduced to Dr Greenslade, who

> started as a doctor in a whaling ship. Then he had been in the
> South African War and afterwards a temporary magistrate
> up Lydenburg way. He soon tired of that, and was for a long
> spell in Uganda and German East, where he became rather
> a swell on tropical diseases ... Then he was in South
> America, where he had a good practice in Valparaiso, and
> then in the Malay States, where he made a bit of money in
> the rubber boom. (9)

This is only about half of the doctor's list of global adventures, which apparently include no other people, yet manage to enrich him enough so he can continue his peripatetic lifestyle without concern for international borders or politics.

This ability to wander the globe is part of being British (Hannay does considerable wandering himself) and white in Buchan's text. The British are 'we who are trying to patch up civilisation' (23) to counter 'the young Bolshevik Jews' (23) and 'the sullen murderous hobbledehoys in Ireland' (23). Buchan's British characters bemoan any attempts at allowing colonial subjects a say in their own destiny: 'The old English way was to regard all foreigners as slightly childish and rather idiotic and ourselves as the only grown-ups in a kindergarten world' (60), one character complains right before a discussion of Gandhi, who is labelled 'a fanatic' (61).

Racism and anti-Semitism are rarely countered in Buchan's text. Julius Victor, for example, is 'one of the richest men in the world' (17) and through his wealth achieves the status of 'the whitest Jew since the Apostle Paul' (17). A character described as 'the man we used to call Ram Dass' (61), even though this is not his name, is useful in getting 'big sums from the agitators and pay[ing] them into the British Exchequer' (62). But even though this Indian person is useful to the British, he is neither given the dignity of his own name nor described as fully human; he is 'wise as a serpent and loyal as a dog' (62). Victor, though Jewish, can earn honorary whiteness through his wealth, but an Indian person cannot even earn the status of full humanity. Buchan's work reflects attitudes of many British people during the Empire about the immutability of power hierarchies that kept white (and Christian) people on top.

However, even Peacock books that appear to question the colonial system remain focused on the needs and concerns of white characters. One of these is the 1963 novella *Walkabout*, in which two white American children crash in the Australian desert and are saved by an Aboriginal boy. The listed author is James Vance Marshall – an Australian-born adventurer who travelled throughout Australia. However, although Marshall gave permission for long descriptive passages from his travel diaries to be used ('Author of *Walkabout* Who Preferred Anonymity'), the actual author was Donald Payne, an Oxford-educated editor and World War II pilot. Although he visited Australia as a child, Payne grew up and lived most of his adult life in England.

Payne's anonymity is important, because Kaye Webb marketed the book as a realistic, true-to-life novel. In *Walkabout*'s front-of-the-book blurb, which Webb wrote, she quotes reviews from the *Observer* and *The Times*, both of which emphasise the truthfulness of the book. The *Observer* critic felt it was 'so compelling that it did not occur to me to doubt its plausibility' (1) and the *Times* critic remarked upon how it was 'filled with information about desert flora and fauna' (1). Most white scholars also reviewed it favourably. Robyn Sheahan-Bright, an Australian critic, calls it 'a lyrical and uncompromising examination of the plight of two white children rescued by a Black boy and their eventual effect on him' (6). David Rees sees it as a damning indictment of racism: 'White civilisation in the book has been tried and found wanting, has bred neurosis' (94). Chambers recommends the book for reluctant teenage readers (*Reluctant Reader* 76). However, the focus of all these reviews is white British readers and characters. This is a story of white children helped by a noble savage – who dies from a minor cold that the white boy gives to him. And yet the last twenty-five pages of *Walkabout* hardly mention the Aboriginal boy at all, and the children are never described as grieving for their friend. The white children kill him by bringing their germs, but 'innocently' because they do not mean to do harm. When he dies, the white children christen him, bury him, and decide he has gone to heaven. In the next scene, their attention has shifted to a platypus playing in a pool. They use skills and knowledge the Aboriginal boy taught them to survive until rescued, but they fail to honour his memory in any substantial way. Like good colonisers, they make the land their own and take from it what they need until they can return to civilisation. Gay Breyley argues that novels like *Walkabout* succeeded because they played into national (and, I would argue, British colonial) myths about Australia in which white children are protected from the wild, while Brown children are ultimately lost:

> The image of the lost child featured in popular representations became an Australian archetype. Pink-skinned children were lost in the bush … If found in time, children were cared for by local heroes, trackers, and/or animals, among others. Meanwhile, generations of brown-skinned children were taken from their families and institutionalised, to 'protect' them from their parents' words and practices. (Breyley 43)

In Marshall's novel, the Aboriginal boy is, like Breyley's institutionalised children, made invisible and easy to forget. The reader is positioned to care only about the safety and well-being of white children; the message is one of survival of the fittest. Webb's early Peacock choices rejected contemporary depictions of people of colour in favour of characters who either accept their place in the racial hierarchy created by European colonisation or, if they reject it, live outside civilisation altogether.

Everyone in Their Place: Non-Fiction in Early Peacocks

The 1960s Peacocks also contained non-fiction titles. Many library surveys had found that teenagers often read non-fiction even if they read nothing else but magazines, and their reading of non-fiction tended to be quite broad. Norman Tomlinson, in a 1963 article for *Library Review*, suggested that librarians were often overwhelmed during school holidays by teen readers asking for non-fiction titles: 'they are voracious readers of anything connected with leisure interests – motor cycles, dancing, hi-fi, sports, railways, photography, instrumental tutors, sheet music, the literature of growing up including etiquette and dress' (100). This broad range of interests indicates how teenagers spent (or wanted to spend) their leisure time, and how leisure activities connected teens with each other through popular culture.

Kaye Webb's choices in non-fiction, however, tended to avoid popular culture altogether; Valerie Grove notes that Webb 'certainly didn't want to deal in books about sex, drugs and rock 'n' roll' (66). In the 1960s, Webb included a few non-fiction titles focused on animals and their relation to people. From books that she had commissioned from children's publishers for Puffin, Webb chose one from Collins to put into Peacock: Gerald Durrell's *The New Noah* (Collins 1955, Peacock 1962), which detailed Durrell's animal-collecting trips around the world. This book would, by 1969, be published by Puffin instead, perhaps indicating Webb's growing understanding of her readership. Two other animal titles were taken from adult (Penguin) lists: J. H. Williams' *Elephant Bill* (Penguin 1956, Peacock 1963) and Jim Corbett's *Man-Eaters of Kumaon* (Penguin 1955, Peacock 1964). These books are both autobiographical accounts of white British soldiers who tame or kill animals in the colonies before and during World War II. Both books are very Eurocentric; the white British author is skilled at killing or training, and everyone else bows to his expertise. The people of India (Corbett) and Burma (Williams) *need* white Europeans to help or save them.

Corbett begins his first chapter by killing a tigress, 'a full-fledged man-eater from Nepal' (16). 'The people of the village', Corbett writes, 'numbering some fifty men, women and children, were in a state of abject terror' (17).

This is, apparently, the only emotion villagers feel, as Corbett goes from village to village saving nameless Indian people from 'a state of terror' (95) or being 'frozen with terror' (134). *Man-Eaters of Kumaon* does not use the racist language of many similar accounts from the Victorian era; the people are 'villagers' and not natives (or worse), for example. But Corbett depicts them as helpless without the British, and comments on their belief in 'charms' (43) and 'evil spirits' (82), as well as their 'superstitious' (185) natures, indicating childlike and primitive people who cannot survive on their own. Corbett speaks of Indians as terrified children, but also as British possessions. He talks of 'our hill folk' (64) and 'the people of our hills' (185) without irony. When the book was originally published, in 1944, this may have been possible (although by then, it was clear that India would soon gain independence). But in 1964, more than fifteen years after India's partition and independence, Webb's choice offers an anachronistic message for white, British readers. Corbett's novel is an argument for the continuation of the British Empire in the Kiplingesque sense of the white man's burden; even when they might want to leave Indian people to their own devices, it would be cruel to do so. Webb could have added some kind of historical note to put Corbett's attitudes in context, but she does not. Indeed, her introductory blurb does not mention Indian *people* at all.

Williams' *Elephant Bill* has similar attitudes towards Burmese people. He calls them 'savage' (135) and 'like school children' (183), given to 'superstitions' (87) and practical jokes. It is only with difficulty and patience that Williams rescues elephants during the Japanese advance on India during World War II. Like Corbett, he is the only one who understands wild animals; he has to issue instructions to Indian people on how to treat elephants, and 'in spite of that, elephants were still kept tied to trees for hours . . . The Gurkha, who is a jolly little man, thought it very funny to be riding an elephant, and it was quite common for me to catch as many as six of them on the back of one animal' (182). There is no sense in either book that people who have lived with wild animals for millennia might have any understanding or knowledge about them; it is only the (white) British who can conquer the wilderness. Williams' story again hearkens back to an earlier, imperial time, and Webb's introductory blurb emphasises this, making Williams seem to be acting alone: 'During the big Japanese advance on India he brought out as many elephants as possible by a new route over precipitous mountain-tracks and through pathless jungle. This feat surpassed Hannibal's crossing of the Alps' (1). Like adventure fiction that Webb published as Peacocks, non-fiction selections underscored white British superiority at a time when the British population was changing and becoming more diverse.

With Peacock Feathers Flying: Involving Teen Readers after 1971

In 1971, Kaye Webb and her staff decided to reinvigorate Peacock by doing something they had not done previously: asking teenage readers what they actually wanted to read. They sent Puffin Club members registered as being fourteen or older a questionnaire. 'We have had a wonderful response to the questionnaire we sent, and the 40 lucky participants will be hearing from us very soon' ('Peacock Questionnaire' 1) about their participation in a 'Peacock Think-In' in September of 1971. By the next issue, it had become 'our famous Peacock Think-In at Bulmershe College, Reading, when 40 older members came to tell us what they want to read *after* they've used up all the Puffins' ('Peacock Think-In' 1). Webb's Puffin Club, with its journal *Puffin Post*, was one of her marketing successes, wherein children paid for the privilege of receiving advertising about new Puffin books four times a year. Valerie Grove notes that when Webb announced the club in March 1967, 'the applications for membership arrived like an avalanche. There were 20,000 members within a couple of months' (60). Although early issues focused primarily on Puffins, by 1970 the *Puffin Post* was including news and competitions for Peacock readers as well, including a 'Design a Cover' competition and a short story competition set by Naomi Lewis. The cover competition was not as much of a success as Webb had hoped; as she commented in announcing the winners, 'Unfortunately most of you sent in your ideas for designs for book covers (very often Puffins not Peacocks) without getting the chief point, which was that we wanted you older readers to think about a *new kind of cover*, to let us know how you really like to see books presented to you' ('Peacock Competition' 24). It is this frustration that may have precipitated Webb's idea to invite some Peacock members to discuss the list in person at Bulmershe College in September 1971.

Unfortunately, very little evidence of what happened at the Think-In remains beyond a few photographs. One of these is a group photograph, with the caption, 'THINK-IN' OVER – with Peacock feathers flying the entire party assembled for a group photograph in the grounds of Bulmershe College of Education, Reading' ('At the Peacock Think-In' 29). The photo depicts what appears to be an all-white group of teenagers. They are well dressed – some of the boys are wearing blazers and several girls are in dresses – suggesting Webb's target middle-class audience was well represented. What the teens discussed was not recorded, and the event (unlike Puffin Club outings and events) was not repeated. While paying lip service to teenagers, Webb never valued Peacock as much as she did Puffin; Lucy Pearson notes, 'While she had responded with energy to the challenges inherent in promoting and developing children's literature, she lacked enthusiasm for a specialist literature for adolescents' (109). Nonetheless, books published as Peacocks did change (albeit slowly) after the Think-In.

Webb's attempts to reach out to new readers went beyond white teenagers. Long-time Lambeth librarian Janet Hill, in *Children are People*, recounts that in 1971

> Rosalind Clark, who had run a successful workshop for children in Edinburgh for five years, had just moved to London, and Kaye Webb of Puffin books had discussed with her the possibility of starting a workshop involving members of the Puffin Club. They had no suitable premises. However, Kaye Webb knew of our plans to make full use of buildings. In April 1971 the first session of the South Island Workshop, a joint Lambeth/Puffin venture was held, starting with a generous grant from the Puffin Club. (61)

Lambeth was, at the time, a largely Black and working-class area of London, and Hill, a white librarian, had spent much of her career championing the needs of Black British child readers. The willingness of Webb to reach out to Hill's readership argues against Valerie Grove's suggestion that Webb 'had little inclination to appeal to ethnic minorities' (66). Yet it is true that Webb's efforts were not always successful, and certainly not in this case; Hill tactfully suggests that 'most of the Puffin Club children have dropped out, because they had to travel long distances to get [to Lambeth], and the workshop has gradually become a local affair' (62). Webb's efforts to interact with new readers did not always work, and attempts at greater inclusion in books published by Peacock after 1970 had equally mixed results.

Once and Future History: Addressing Enslavement in Peacocks

One way that Webb could have easily addressed racial diversity in Peacock books was through the historical treatment of the British trade in enslaved people. Webb clearly valued historical fiction, but most of her choices did not address Britain's transatlantic slave trade, even in an opaque way. In fact, in Peacock novels before 1975, slavery is not associated with Britain at all, existing only outside of Britain, as in Géza Gárdonyi's Hungarian classic, taken from Penguin's adult list, *Slave of the Huns* (1973) and Robert Heinlein's science fiction work *Citizen of the Galaxy* (1972).

Gárdonyi's novel, originally published in Hungary in 1901 (first published in Britain by Dent in 1969), is about life in Attila the Hun's military. The Greek-born protagonist, Zeta, is enslaved, but has not been kidnapped and forced into slavery. He *chooses* slavery in order to try to distinguish himself in front of Emmo, a Hun princess. Heinlein's *Citizen of the Galaxy* also features an enslaved protagonist. Thorby, at the beginning of Heinlein's novel, is sold at auction. Originally written in 1957, amid debates over African-American civil rights in America, the novel discusses many aspects of slavery. But Thorby is not African-American, and he has many advantages that enslaved Africans did not have. He is owned by a man, Baslim, who appears to be a beggar but is actually a spy, involved in tracking down pirates involved in the slave trade. He frees Thorby against his will; the first time Baslim suggests it, Thorby says, 'Pop, I *like* belonging to you' (25). Thorby continues to protest his manumission and refuses to leave Baslim, who eventually adopts and teaches him. 'Baslim had long since taught Thorby to read and write Sargonese and Interlingua' (28); by the time Baslim dies, Thorby can speak seven languages and is fit to become a Free Trader. Perhaps the books gave white readers a way of imagining themselves as enslaved, but neither Gárdonyi's book about slavery in the Hun empire nor Heinlein's book about enslaved white people in space substitute for historical fiction about Africans enslaved by Britons in the Empire.

Down the Garden Path: Sex across Racial Lines in 1970s Peacocks

By the late 1970s, Kaye Webb's interest in books for teenagers had flagged. Where Puffin had been a phenomenal success, Peacock had never really gotten off the ground. Many more children read regularly than teens, and without addressing issues of interest to teens – popular culture, sexuality, and relationships with the wider world – Peacock only appealed to a small group of the most literate, and mostly white, British teenagers. In 1977, Webb turned over day-to-day control of Peacock to Dorothy Wood (joined, slightly later, by Tony Lacey), who relaunched Peacock in a bid to appeal more widely. Wood's and Lacey's Peacocks pushed the boundaries of what Webb found acceptable reading, particularly in terms of teen sex and popular culture. However, while more of the world came into novels published in Peacock, the main focus remained the white British teen, and Britain remained a space racialised as white.

Marjorie Darke's *The First of Midnight* (1977) is an ideal example of how Peacock changed – and did not change – after Webb stepped back from day-to-day oversight. This book, like many that Peacock published about Black and white interaction, centres on the white character. As I write elsewhere, 'it is the white character who is introduced first, and who is the most fully developed' (*Soon Come Home* 109). Jess, a white servant, and Midnight, an enslaved Black man who boxes to earn money for his freedom, become friendly because they share in common the fact that freedom for people like them is limited in England. Both the working-class and the enslaved person have to answer to everyone else. By linking the fate of poor white and enslaved Black people, Darke may provide a way for white readers to connect with the history of slavery. But like *Slave of the Huns* and *Citizen of the Galaxy*, *The First of Midnight*'s concern with white characters keeps readers from engaging fully with the horrors of the historical British transatlantic slave trade.

The book also showcases another way in which Peacock developed after Dorothy Wood assumed primary editorship over the imprint: the inclusion of sexual or romantic relationships across racial lines. Open inclusion of sexual relationships was not something that Kaye Webb had been comfortable with in Peacock, because it caused (white) parents to complain. Felicity Trotman notes that even '*Walkabout* by James Vance Marshall was regularly criticised – for its acceptance of nudity . . . and also when it first came out because there is a suggestion that the white girl Mary might quite like the black boy' (75). But Mary's supposed attraction to the unnamed Aboriginal boy who saves them manifests outwardly only in hostility, and she barely seems to remember him after he dies. Peacock books published in the late 1970s contain white characters who openly acknowledge attraction to characters outside their racial group, and either think about or enter into sexual relationships with those characters. In addition to *The First of Midnight*, Peacocks published in 1977 included Elizabeth Kata's *A Patch of Blue* (first UK pub. Michael Joseph 1961), Rumer Godden's *The Peacock Spring* (orig. pub. Macmillan 1975), and Julius Lester's *Basketball Game* (first UK pub. Kestrel 1974). Description of sex in these novels is circumspect and sometimes metaphoric. Jessica Yates points out that Peacock's editors had 'a failure of nerve' (183) when it came to sex, and the cross-racial relationships portrayed in these books are ultimately doomed, underscoring fears and stereotypes held by white Britons about Black and Asian men and miscegenation. Darke's and Godden's books, which include direct if non-specific descriptions of sex and pregnancies resulting from relationships, showcase these fears and stereotypes most clearly.

Godden was an unsurprising choice for publication in Peacock. Godden's doll stories (such as *The Doll's House* or *Miss Happiness and Miss Flower*) had been published in the 1960s and early 1970s in Puffin, so she was an author that Webb trusted. Godden had also published novels, some reprinted by Penguin, based on her experiences growing up in India. However, *The Peacock Spring* had only been published two years before, by Macmillan, and was not (as so many of Webb's choices were) taken from the Penguin or Puffin lists. It tells the story of two schoolgirls, Una who is fifteen and her twelve-year-old half-sister Hal, who have been summoned from their boarding school to live with their father, a UN diplomat, in India. He tells Una it is because he wants 'someone to read with and talk to again' (17), but it quickly becomes clear that their presence in India is to regularise their father's relationship with a 'Eurasian' woman named Alix Lamont. Alix officially becomes their governess, but is badly schooled, so Una seeks additional help in mathematics. One of the gardeners is an Indian named Ravi, who has taken the position to give him time to write his poetry in peace; he and Una fall in love during his mathematics tutoring.

White writers published by Peacock portrayed sex across racial lines with an exoticism that added to the need for the relationship to be doomed. The idea of Black and Asian people as sexually interesting to white Britons goes back hundreds of years. Edward Said called sensuality one of 'the essential aspects of the . . . Oriental character' (203) for the British and other imperialist nations. Miranda Kaufmann discusses white British ideas about Black sexuality in the Tudor period in her chapter on 'Anne Cobbie, the Tawny Moor with Soft Skin' in *Black Tudors*. Gretchen Holbrook Gerzina comments that in the eighteenth century, 'despite everyday interactions between blacks and whites, discussion about black women and white men quickly degenerated to its lowest sexual denominator' (71). And David Olusoga suggests that 'opposition to inter-racial relationships' was a factor in the race riots of 1919 (459). While relationships across racial lines were common throughout history, they were not seen as permanent but as a rite of passage, especially for the white coloniser. Godden has Una describe herself as 'like the girls in the Keats poem, "creeping thin with lust"' (181). Gregory Wassil discusses 'Keats' Orientalism' as 'participating in a major cultural displacement outward into empire and encounters with otherness' (422), so Godden's use of the quotation is appropriate; Una has been displaced from her home, and her encounters with otherness allow her to move from childhood to adulthood.

Encounters with otherness, however, are more risky for women than for men. Godden sets the scene for Una's doom by indicating the vast web of lies Alix has spun in order to cover a past of being an abandoned wife and, subsequently, the unmarriageable mistress of several high-ranking Indian men. Alix's heritage, however, and not her previous marriage, is what turns Indian society against her. She calls herself 'the girl without a chance – half-caste' (229). She loves Vikram Singh, a son of a Maharajah, and he loves her – but cannot marry her because his family wants him to 'make pure-bred Rajput' (203) heirs. The need for racial purity was an attitude that dominated in Britain as well; Charlie Owen notes in 2001 that 'while opinion polls and attitude surveys going back to the 1950s show an increasing acceptance of mixed marriages in Britain, there is still continuing hostility' (135). Jayne O. Ifekwunigwe in 'Re-membering "Race"' attributes this hostility to white Britons: 'there is still a deep-seated and now unspoken White English anxiety concerning "racial" infiltration by Black and Asian "alien-settlers"' (58). Webb's middle-class white readers might be given stories about cross-racial relationships, but they could not end in happy families.

Una enters into adulthood in part because of her awareness of her stepmother's past as an unmarriageable mistress. Prior to *Peacock Spring*'s initial sex scene, Una has just been whipped by her stepmother for threatening to expose Alix's affair with a high-ranking Indian. This violent act opens Una up; both physically, giving her open welts on her skin, and figuratively 'opening her eyes' to the lengths Alix will go to keep her past secret. The physical wounding of Una gives her Indian lover Ravi the excuse to touch and care for her but also to worry that he may hurt her:

> 'Touch me. Come closer.'
> 'But . . . if I hurt your back.'
> 'Let it hurt. Oh Ravi! Come close.' (Godden 180)

This is the entire description of their encounter, but two pages later, Una has become experienced and 'love with Ravi does not hurt me any more' (182). By displacing pain of sexual penetration with Una's open wounds, Godden can metaphorically depict Una's lustful desire as a love that will hurt her.

Marjorie Darke's description of the sexual encounter between Jess and Midnight is more graphic, but it also plays on stereotypes about why white women desire Black men. Described from Jess' perspective, she moves from 'all the old fears' (159) to a feeling that 'even the discomfort as he drove into her was a small price to pay for the abandoned animal joy' (159). Like Una, she accepts the pain of him 'driving into' her; this is not the description of a gentle first love but of an encounter of 'animal joy'. Catherine Hall notes in *Civilising Subjects* that an 'animal-like sexuality of black men' (258) was a common stereotype held by white Britons, but Darke and Godden reverse this stereotype. In Darke's novel, it is Jess who becomes animal. The sexual interaction with Jess for Midnight, on the other hand, 'allowed him to be a man' (Darke 159). Ravi, too, matures into manhood, winning a national poetry prize following his relationship with Una. Sex with white women allows Ravi and Midnight to become men; sex for Una and Jess, however, means a kind of degeneration into animal lust. Una tries, and fails, to convince Ravi to marry her; she then becomes literally outcast, from India and from the adult world, sent back to boarding school in England following the abortion. *The First of Midnight* ends with Midnight returning to Africa without his pregnant lover, who finds a home with a kindly white abolitionist. The young protagonists' pregnancies do not lead them into adulthood, but return them both to a state of dependency on older, white adults.

Peacock books after 1970 are more likely to depict emotional attachment between white Britons and Black and Asian people. However, the focus is almost entirely on the experience of and consequences for the white (and generally female) character. While Black and Asian characters gain self-knowledge, status, and security, white characters face loss of position, home, and family to interact with lovers outside their racial group. Taken as a whole, Peacock books published in the 1970s suggest sympathy towards their presumed-white reader in desiring friendship and affection with Black and Asian people – but they also act as a warning, that such relationships are a risk, and that the risk belongs primarily to white characters in a post-imperial world.

So You Want to Be a Part of Britain? Peacock Non-Fiction after 1977

In a study done in British libraries in 1975, 'more than half the loans' (M. Marshall 236) from teen sections of libraries were non-fiction. Undoubtedly some loans related to young adults' school work, but Marshall insists on the importance for all teens of having a wide non-fiction selection relating to interests: 'books of biography, sociology, hobbies, personal matters in the sense of psychology, health, grooming, sex and dating, sport and travel' (227) should join career-orientated books on teen shelves. The big game hunting in the Empire books published early on by Peacock did not satisfy either teen hobbyists or career investigators, and the cookery book 'especially for girls' felt outdated by the late 1970s. Kaye Webb had long resisted the popular and trendy – she told the Associated Booksellers of New Zealand in 1964 that 'many parents think that if children learn to read they will look after themselves, but this is not true' ('Need to Wean Children' 2); she suggested that 'children would never progress' from the popular 'unless someone helped them' (2). Peacock books, including non-fiction, were designed to help readers 'explore the more adult world' (2) and not the world of pop music, dating, or sport.

Even after Webb stepped back from primary involvement in Peacock, her influence remained strong. Although Dorothy Wood and Tony Lacey, who took over editing responsibility for Peacock after the imprint's relaunch, embraced popular culture and hobbies in a way that Kaye Webb never did, the books were still aimed at a predominantly white audience. The gendered nature of early Peacock non-fiction disappeared (at least to some extent); Felicity Trotman notes that Janet Allen's *Fashion for Free* (1979) 'included things boys could do, and you didn't necessarily need to sew!' (79). On the other hand, some Peacock non-fiction continued to be targeted towards boys only, including Eamon Dunphy's *Only a Game? The Diary of a Professional Footballer* (1977). Dunphy's diary was edited by *Time Out* journalist Peter Ball, who he says 'rescued the unwieldy mass of taped and written material from my dustbin to shape it into a book' (14). However, Dunphy would go on to be a *Times* journalist himself, and Ian Ridley called him 'a brave, lyrical Celtic writer'. Dunphy's book details the end of his football career at Millwall, as he becomes increasingly disillusioned in 1973–4. That the book attempts to give a fairly honest account of football in the 1970s is evident in Dunphy's open criticism of specific coaches and players, whether from his team or not. But even though he describes himself in the book's introduction as 'a snide, bigoted little man' (14), there is no evidence in the book that Dunphy was racially bigoted.

Indeed, there is no evidence that he thought about racism at all, because the book mentions no Black players.

But Dunphy played for Millwall, which, as he himself wrote elsewhere, was known as 'synonymous with . . . football hooliganism' ('Millwall vs the Mob'). The year that Peacock published Dunphy's book, Millwall fans were the subject of a BBC *Panorama* episode, in which members of football supporter gangs admitted to participating in National Front activities ('Millwall 1977' 25'28"). Neither hooliganism nor racism make an appearance anywhere in Dunphy's book, even during his discussion of the preseason match against West Ham, who employed Clyde Best and Ade Coker, Black players who regularly faced banana missiles and monkey noises at matches from racist fans. It is possible Best and Coker did not play during the match because of Millwall's reputation. But Dunphy's avoidance of a discussion of racism in football suggests it was not an issue that mattered to him, or that he thought would interest his readers. Kaye Webb may not have been aware of any of this, and only wanted a sports biography suitable for middle-class white readers. Even if she was aware of Millwall's links with hooliganism and racist political groups, she would not have chosen a book for Peacock readers that discussed these things, especially not amid growing tensions in England over racial issues.

Even Webb could not entirely ignore the ways that Britain was changing by the late 1970s. Teenagers and schoolchildren were recruited for political activities, including School Kids Against Nazis (SKAN) and Rock Against Racism, two organisations that allowed young people to discuss racism in creative and critical forums. Peacock's response to both readers' desires to think about their future careers and their increasing political activity was Des Wilson's *So You Want to Be Prime Minister: An Introduction to British Politics Today* (1979). The book's cover stood out from other Peacock non-fiction, which typically used photography only, by being a collage of photography and cartoon-like drawings. This allows for readers to better imagine themselves in the picture, because surrounding the black-and-white photograph of Number Ten Downing Street are colour drawings of young people carrying signs with various requests for voter support. The young people represented are mostly white, but there are at least two ethnic minorities on the cover. No one person on the cover dominates, and the suggestion is clear: all British young people have the right to aim for prime minister. This marks a definite change from the tiger hunting and elephant training books Peacock offered readers initially, which maintained imperial racial hierarchies.

The emphasis on race and racial issues continues inside Wilson's book, but in a way that is clearly aimed at Webb's white middle-class reader. In the chapter 'We the Voters', Wilson comments: 'Another, and particularly sad, influence on British elections in recent years has been the question of race' (48). Wilson goes on to discuss various examples of white politicians using race to further their careers: the Smethwick campaign of 1964 (though he did not mention the infamous racist campaign slogan of this election); Enoch Powell's 'Rivers of Blood' speech, which called for the return of Black people to the Caribbean; and Margaret Thatcher's 1978 *Panorama* appearance in which she discussed (white) British people feeling 'swamped' by people of colour. Wilson concludes, 'It is a sad fact that in a country that prides itself on tolerance, prejudice on race cannot be ruled out as a factor that can swing votes in some parts of the country. It is also a sad fact that there are politicians who will take advantage of this' (50). Racism is depicted negatively, but without describing racism's effects on actual Black and Brown people. The index does not include entries for race, racism, or even immigration, although abortion (215), the Miners' strike (216), and Scottish Nationalists (217) are all included. Wilson's book urges white readers to be 'tolerant' of other people, but does not suggest that racism is a problem for them; only for the 'sad' victims of racism. Peacock non-fiction after 1977 undergoes a dramatic change from a focus on colonial adventure to British-focused activities and events – but it still does not recognise racism as a problem for all Britain's citizens.

Peacock, Plus and Minus: The End of Peacock

Kaye Webb retired in 1979, and soon after, books that had been published in Peacock became 'Puffin Plus' books instead. Peacock had survived seventeen years and two attempts to reinvent it, but it had never had the success that Puffin had; by placing teen books back under Puffin's auspices, the editors (Wood and Lacey) may have been trying to revive this area of their publishing. But by labelling the books Puffin Plus, they also anchored them more firmly to childhood publishing instead of adult publishing. Linda Lloyd Jones notes that 'the series suffered from the fact that the category of adolescent publishing was a new one and therefore booksellers had not recognised place in which to display it' (71–2). However, YA books and imprints continued long after Peacock ended. A more likely explanation is the cavernous niche that Webb dug in creating the ideal Peacock audience: a white, middle-class, already-reading audience who accepted ideas about gender and racial hierarchies established long before they were born. Pearson notes that Webb believed the teenager who was a 'fluent and enthusiastic reader' (109) would prefer adult books anyway. Although there is some evidence that Webb tried to appeal to other readers, through Puffin Club activities in Lambeth, she seems to have had little understanding of any teenagers, let alone the Black and Asian teens, who by 1979 formed the majority of potential readers in several areas of London, Birmingham, Manchester, and other British cities. By failing to take into account her audience, Webb's experiment with YA literature ultimately failed.

Crossover Text: G. M. Glaskin's *A Waltz through the Hills*

In 1961, G. M. Glaskin's children's novel, *A Waltz through the Hills*, was one of the submissions for the prestigious Miles Franklin Literary Award, given to the novel with literary merit that best presented Australian life in any given year. The novel did not win, perhaps because it was of a familiar pattern for Australian novels. Like *Walkabout*, which I discussed in the previous chapter, Glaskin's novel concerns two white children travelling alone (in this case their parents died and the children are trying to reach their English grandparents), who are saved from starvation and other disasters by an Aboriginal person. Glaskin's Aboriginal character, unlike Marshall's, has a name (Frank Smith), speaks English and is otherwise 'civilised', making the relationship between him and the children much more interactive than that found in *Walkabout*. As well as being published in Australia, the novel was simultaneously published in England by adult publishing house Barrie and Rockliff (whose best-known author was P. G. Wodehouse). It was then picked up by both New Windmill (in 1964) and Peacock (in 1970). However, when Kaye Webb published it in Peacock, she did not publish the entire text, but a revised version. An analysis of both versions indicates a great deal about racial attitudes in Britain at the time, but also demonstrates the different publishing ethos of the editors.

Glaskin's book, unlike *Walkabout*, places Aboriginal people within society's bounds, although they must choose either to live in poverty on the fringes of white-majority towns or on reservations. Stereotypically, they drink alcohol to excess and are often involved in petty crime, but Glaskin suggests that it is marginalisation by white people that causes these problems. When Andy, a white boy, finds out that Frank has been imprisoned three times, he is surprised. 'He thought only wicked people went to gaol, like murderers and thieves and other kinds of criminals. But Frank didn't seem to be any of these' (186 New Windmill/183 Peacock). But Frank says that he stole chickens because 'there were a lot of mouths to feed. The welfare money just didn't go nowhere' (187 New Windmill/184 Peacock). When Andy complains that it is not fair, Frank tells him:

maybe when you're grown up, young 'un, you might feel
like doin' something about it, for us folks. There sure aren't
many as are doin' it now. Fact most people just seem to think
we shouldn't be here at all. Guess they forget the black side
of us was here first, and we're only coloured as they call us
because the whites wanted a – a certain amount to do with
us – or with our womenfolks, rather (189 New Windmill).

The novel depicts Frank, not as a criminal, but as someone who commits
criminal acts in an institutionally racist system.

This last quotation is from the New Windmill edition, and highlights one
difference between Serraillier's editing and Kaye Webb's. In Webb's version,
the quotation stops at 'Guess they forget the black side of us was here first' (184
Peacock). Webb removed several passages that suggest sexual situations,
including a long segment about sexual rivalry between two teachers at the
children's school. However, while that passage was not relevant to the overall
storyline (and in fact the teachers disappear from the text after the first hundred
pages), passages relating to sex and the Aboriginal population are critical to the
novel's themes. In addition to this passage, which gives Frank greater motiva-
tion for his violence against white men harassing his sister, another passage
that Serraillier left in and Webb excised discusses the differing appearances of
Frank's brothers and sisters. There is a baby whose 'skin looked nearly white'
(171 New Windmill/169 Peacock); and two girls, one whose 'hair was red, her
skin a little darker than the baby's, but with freckles all over it' (172 New
Windmill/169 Peacock) and one who 'was very dark, but had blonde hair'
(172 New Windmill). Webb has removed the description of the blonde sister,
and also the passage that follows, where Frank's mother suggests she is not
sure how many fathers her children have, and that she has never been married.
On its own, this passage might suggest that Frank's mother had rather looser
morals than might be expected of a 'good' mother character in a children's
book, which is perhaps why Webb excised it. However, combined with the
section about white men wanting 'a certain amount to do' with Aboriginal
women, this passage emphasises inequalities of the Australian system, in which
white men need not take responsibility for children they father with Aboriginal
women. Aboriginal mothers are then expected to make do with meagre

welfare money offered by the government, or see their children jailed for stealing food. Webb's changes to Glaskin's text reduce institutional responsibility of the white Australian government towards Aboriginal Australians, instead making racism the individual response of a few 'bad apples'.

Neither edition excises racist language against Aboriginal people used throughout the text by multiple characters. The 'n' word is used frequently as a racist slur, and Aboriginal women are routinely described in negative terms as unusually fat. Intriguingly, negative language about white people has been altered – not in the Peacock edition, but in Serraillier's New Windmill edition. When the children first meet Frank, they try to steal his food. In the New Windmill edition, Frank calls them 'white devils' (148) whereas in the Peacock edition, he calls them 'white bastards' (144). Because New Windmill published for the schools market, one might assume that this language change – the only one that Serraillier made in the entire text – was due to language unacceptable in schools. He often wrote to authors asking them to allow the removal of 'bastard' and 'bloody'. However, New Windmill also published E. R. Braithwaite's *To Sir, with Love* (1971), and in this novel, white teens congratulate a white classmate 'for "putting the black bastard in his place"' (66). Small editorial changes such as these reveal what is acceptable in terms of racially based language. Frank Smith has as much right to chastise the white children as he does the white man who harasses his sister; they are, after all, attempting to steal from him. However, Serraillier's change softens Frank's character, allowing the reader and child characters to be more quickly sympathetic to him.

While there are many differences between Peacock and New Windmill as publishing imprints, revisions made by both Webb and Serraillier to Glaskin's *A Waltz through the Hills* suggest that one key difference is in how racism and racial difference is represented. Webb's choices of books for Peacock that featured Black, Asian, or minority ethnic characters consistently focused on the well-being and moral virtue of white society and white readers. Racism, for Webb, was not a structural feature of British (or white-dominated colonial) society. Serraillier, on the other hand, used New Windmills to question existent power hierarchies – including racial hierarchies. His choices indicate a different understanding of teen readers – not as people who needed guidance and protection, but as potential actors for change.

2 To Know Which Way the Wind Is Blowing: Ian Serraillier and New Windmill

In 1944, the British government began to draw up plans for post-war education to help build Britain's children into citizens of the future. The project's architect, Labour MP Ellen Wilkinson, focused on moral and physical well-being of children more than specific curriculum, which was left to local councils to determine. As I have written elsewhere, this lack of curricular direction in the 1944 act 'gave publishers who concentrated on educational material both considerable freedom to shape curriculum and a new imperative to publish' (*Children's Publishing* 28). In terms of the secondary literature curriculum, however, change was slow. Traditionally, students had been offered a selection of canonical literature written prior to the twentieth century, mostly by white and middle- or upper-class men. But the changing school population – changing in terms of numbers, class, and racial background – meant that students did not respond to the canon as well as they had before (if indeed, the majority ever did). One schoolteacher who had experienced this rejection of school-based reading was Ian Serraillier, who in the late 1940s was teaching English at Midhurst Grammar School.

Midhurst Grammar, in West Sussex, had produced some well-known students (H. G. Wells was a pupil) but by 1944 it was in being run by the local county council and was no longer a boarding school. Tony Beal notes that when Midhurst advertised for an English teacher, the 'enlightened head had specified that he should also be "a practicing writer"' (A17). Serraillier had published two children's books in 1946, and would go on to publish over thirty more. At Midhurst Grammar, he 'particularly enjoyed teaching the younger ones to whom books could be all pleasure' (Beal A17). He wanted all young people to feel similar pleasure, and so he proposed to Heinemann a series of books that 'publishers sell direct to schools – thus being able to produce hard cover books at paperback prices' ('Fiction of Their Time' 14).

Serraillier was particularly keen to publish twentieth-century fiction, but despite his interest in modern fiction, he did not at first take too many risks. Many books on his first list were turn-of-the-century fiction that had already gained 'classic' status – including H. G. Wells' *The Time Machine*, Jack

London's *The Call of the Wild*, and Frances Hodgson Burnett's *The Secret Garden*. Non-fiction titles included biographies by Eleanor Doorly, including her Carnegie Medal-winning *Radium Woman* about Marie Curie; and retellings of Greek myths.

Yet even his early list was not without innovation. He published Eve Garnett's *Family from One-End Street*, which was about working-class Britons. Although the book had won the Carnegie Medal in 1938, and had been published in Penguin Puffins by Kaye Webb's predecessor Eleanor Graham in 1942, it was a radical departure from traditional depictions of working-class families, particularly those depicted in school-based texts. Kim Reynolds notes that Garnett's 'characters are based on first-hand observation of real children and families' (155) and, because the book was aimed at a middle-class audience, it 'provided a corrective to the perception that poor children came from degenerate stock and were unfit for the nation's needs' (156). By choosing to put *One-End Street* into New Windmill (despite it arguably being pitched at a younger audience), Serraillier directed the book towards a potentially much wider readership. It would continue to work as a window, to use Rudine Sims Bishop's metaphor, to the working-class world for middle-class readers, but it might also provide a mirror for working-class readers to see themselves represented positively in books.

Mary Whitehead, head of Heinemann's post-war children's lists, commented on how the publisher did not immediately recognise the needs of the teenage reader, writing that 'no modern teenager would look at some of the books we published' (St John 379). Serraillier's New Windmill series is generally celebrated (including in company histories) because 'thanks to the New Windmill Series, vast numbers of school children have been introduced to the works of D. H. Lawrence, Doris Lessing, George Orwell, Graham Greene, Henry James, H. G. Wells, J. B. Priestley, Roald Dahl, Camus, Hemingway, Masefield, Solzhenitsyn, and many others' (St John 381) – in short, because YA readers were introduced to adult literature. But often, the real innovation of New Windmill came in publishing literature written specifically for teenagers. Although, like Peacock, New Windmill was primarily a reprint publisher (that is to say, Serraillier bought rights to books already published), his choices, unlike Webb's, showed an awareness of modern teenage concerns, and a list that reached beyond middle-class readers to 'not-yet' readers, non-readers, and once-and-future readers. Because of its position as a schools publisher, New Windmill offered books to reach many demographic groups, and this meant that racism and stories with Black and Brown characters appeared earlier and more regularly than they had in Peacock.

The Wide World of Reading: Early New Windmills

Early New Windmills, those published before 1967, tended to look outwards from England to the colonised and formerly colonised world. Like early Peacocks, these books were written by white (and often English) authors who had spent at least part of their lives in colonial settings. Also like early Peacocks, these books were not written specifically for teenage readers; most came from adult lists at Heinemann. While later books would come from writers in Heinemann's specialist New African Writers and Caribbean Writers series, many early New Windmills were focalised through white protagonists and (like some of the early Peacocks) included conflict between white English/European people and Black or Brown 'native' people. Serraillier's choices often, though not always, questioned the centrality and moral correctness of European/English society in the world; unlike many of Kaye Webb's Peacocks, New Windmill books were rarely nostalgic for Empire.

One of the earliest New Windmills chosen to address reluctant readers is also one that introduces a wider world to the (presumably mostly-white, given its original publication date in the imprint) teenage reader: Armstrong Sperry's *The Boy Who Was Afraid* (Bodley Head 1942; New Windmill 1952). Originally published in the United States as *Call It Courage* (Simon and Schuster 1940), it won the Newbery Medal for best children's book of 1941. Sperry, a white American, lived in Polynesia in the 1920s, and set his best-known book there, about a boy who was afraid of the sea. The book had initially been published for children; Sheila Ray lists it as suitable for seven- to nine-year-olds in *Children's Fiction: A Handbook for Librarians* (175). In his Newbery Medal acceptance speech, however, Sperry indicates the uncertainty that many reviewers and publishers felt about the target audience for the book: 'I had been afraid that perhaps in *Call It Courage*, the concept of a spiritual courage might be too adult for children, but the reception of this book has reaffirmed a belief I have long held: that children have imagination enough to grasp any idea, and respond to it' ('Newbery Acceptance Speech'). Aidan Chambers, however, writes that 'because it handles a sympathetic theme (cowardice turned to courage), and is finally told through action . . . it enjoys a readership far greater than originally intended' (*Reluctant Reader* 57). The 'spiritual courage' that Sperry mentions is 'a theme [that] makes even more sense at 15 than it does at 8' (58), according to Chambers. Serraillier's early choices, including many titles originally published on children's lists, encouraged teenagers to read, or perhaps read again, fiction and non-fiction that was not written for them, but had ideas that could challenge their thinking and encourage further reading.

The Boy Who Was Afraid is, like many books about other cultures written by white authors, ambivalent about the depiction of racial and cultural difference. On the one hand, Sperry introduces language and cultural traditions of Hikueru, the small island in French Polynesia, in generally positive fashion. The Hikueru people's language is often inserted without translation, even when it cannot be completely understood from context. For example, the title character Mafatu sings when he feels he has been courageous, 'a brave song of Taaroa, the hero-god who rose out of the sea to slay the enemies of his people' (38). The four-line song is not translated, which puts the Hikueru language on par with English. This may seem a small thing, but often in children's books written during this period, language is used as a weapon to indicate racial hierarchy; Sperry's respectful use also allows the reader scope for either imagination (to determine what the song is about) or further research.

On the other hand, Mafatu is never physically described, nor are other members of his family or tribe. Yet the cannibalistic tribe who use the island where Mafatu is kidnapped *are* described – and they are 'savages' (36) and 'figures as black as night's own face, darting, shifting, bounding toward the sky. The eaters-of-men . . .' (66). Presumably, Mafatu's people are also dark-skinned, but Sperry, by leaving this description out, associates Black skin with fear and savagery, rather than heroics. Sperry's novel would be joined by other award-winning island/shipwreck stories on the New Windmill list, including Scott O'Dell's *Island of the Blue Dolphins* and Theodore Taylor's *The Cay* which also faced criticism for their racial depictions (see, for example, Diann L. Baecker's 'Surviving Rescue: A Feminist Reading of Scott O'Dell's *Island of the Blue Dolphins*'; Carole Goldberg's 'A Counterstory of Native American Persistence'; Susan C. Griffiths' '"So the Very Young Know and Understand": Reframing Discussion of *The Cay*'). These books could all be described as Albert Schwartz, vice-president of the Council on Interracial Books for Children, described *The Cay* in 1970: 'an adventure story for white colonialists' (*'The Cay*: Racism Rewarded' 45). Schwartz's commentary came three years before Serraillier published Taylor's book, but the criticism did not receive widespread attention until *The Cay* was made into a television play in 1974 (Banfield20). Nonetheless, all three books remained available in New Windmill until at least 1982.

Significantly, these island stories were all international award-winners. Publishers, particularly for the educational market, respond to demands of teachers and librarians as well as (perhaps more than) their target audience. Serraillier was no exception; he had to curry favour with education professionals if his imprint were to survive. Teachers and librarians expected to be able to buy award-winning books for leisure reading in their school and classroom libraries, and *The Boy Who Was Afraid*, *The Cay*, and *The Island of the Blue Dolphins* filled this need. But Serraillier also made choices that indicated he had his teenage readers in mind as well, choosing books that would not normally be considered 'educational'. Genre fiction, such as mysteries and Westerns, was largely dismissed by educationalists as simplistic and not literary enough for school reading. Teenagers, on the other hand, ranked these genres quite high on their list of preferences (M. Marshall 62). Serraillier considered it important to include genre fiction in New Windmill to entice teenage readers, but chose books that challenged typical genre expectations, particularly about race. Arthur Upfield's *Bony and the Mouse* (Heinemann 1959; New Windmill 1961) and John Prebble's *The Buffalo Soldiers* (Secker and Warburg 1959; New Windmill 1965) are two books that suggest that Serraillier hoped to use genre fiction to question prevailing attitudes about racism and colonialism in Britain. They also show Serraillier's progression on racial issues as the country became more and more multiracial.

Bony and the Mouse was the twenty-sixth of thirty stories written by Arthur Upfield about his Australian detective Nat Bonnar, nicknamed Napoleon Bonaparte or Bony. Nineteen of these were published by Heinemann in their adult lists. Upfield, English by birth, had spent considerable time in Australia and was married to an Australian. This particular title was the first mystery Serraillier published, and he did not publish any other Bony stories (he did go on to publish Graham Greene's *The Third Man* and Alfred Hitchcock's *Sinister Spies* in the early 1970s). If Serraillier had wanted to publish mysteries, he could easily have chosen more well-known authors: the Perry Mason stories on Heinemann's lists, or some Edgar Allen Poe stories if he wanted something 'literary' enough for an educational imprint. Upfield was an unusual choice for Serraillier and an unusual author for his time. St John notes that 'Upfield was rare among Australian writers in his feeling for the Aborigines; indeed, his books possess an anthropological value quite apart from their merits as mystery thrillers' (357). Upfield's protagonist, Bony, had a white father and an Aboriginal mother, unique in detective fiction up to this point. This centring of Aboriginal characters made the novel useful for Serraillier's aims.

Late twentieth and early twenty-first century critics are clear that Upfield's depiction is problematic. Lucy Sussex writes in her review of a documentary about Upfield, 'In Search of Bony', that 'Bony was quite impossible for his times, as a university-educated Aboriginal detective policeman ... Upfield was purveying a fantasy, but with immense believability' (98). Daniel Walden adds that 'from time to time, stereotypes creep in. Bony's instincts, primitive instincts, describe Aboriginal behaviour' (173). He also points out that white Australian characters frequently use racial slurs to describe Aboriginal people. In Serraillier's edited version, stereotypes remain, but racial slurs were slightly modified for schools. Although he changed terminology, it was generally to remove swear words such as 'bloody' and 'bastard'. 'Black bastards', a phrase which appears in both books originally, becomes 'Black swine' or 'Black devils', removing some of the racial slur's force but not the focus on skin colour.

Critics admire Upfield's work despite the slurs and stereotypes; Walden called Bony 'extraordinary' (173) and 'a bridge between two cultures' (173) – a feature that makes *Bony and the Mouse* ideal for New Windmill, which tried to reach multiple audiences and raise awareness of different cultures and ideas. Bony is quick to defend Aboriginal people against stereotypes, as he tells a nurse: 'Your aunt informed me that you have been wasting your fresh young life for three years by working among these awful bush people . . . Her words, not mine. I defended you and the awful bush people' (42). Upfield also has other characters defending them: Tony Carr, who is accused (but innocent) of the book's murders, comments that the Aboriginal people 'are decent blokes in their own way' (61); and the bar owner, Melody Sam, says that 'they call 'em savages, they call 'em this and that, but they're the only decent people living in the world today . . . I don't hold with forcing them people into our own dirty, murderous, sinful state we call civilisation' (86–7). Bony agrees with Sam's statement, but also holds himself apart from the Aboriginal people, despite his mother's background. He talks to them in Hollywood Indian speech: 'killum-feller he come like Kurdatia and basham your lubra . . . This killing plenty bad' (101); he cannot speak the native tongue. But he has their 'natural' tracking ability, an ability described in the book as both magical and animal-like. Aboriginal trackers, according to one character, could read foot tracks so well that they 'could have told me what the feller et for dinner, or got close to it' (82). Bony himself tracks like a cat; Upfield notes that 'much of the cat's psychology had been bequeathed to Inspector Bonaparte by his aboriginal mother, a member of a race which down the ladder of the centuries had had to cultivate feline patience if it were to survive' (164). Bony not only survived, he thrived, by embracing his father's culture and his mother's nature. Despite rejecting his mother's society, he defends Aborigines against not only racism, but cultural genocide in the form of white 'civilisation' efforts.

A few years later, Serraillier published another work of genre fiction, John Prebble's Western *The Buffalo Soldiers*. The book contains a much more complicated depiction of race and racism than others that Serraillier had published. Prebble, a white English writer, was best known in his lifetime for writing about the Highland clearances, where English soldiers used brutal force to drive Scottish people from their land; his *Buffalo Soldiers* shows similar sympathy for powerless Americans. Certainly it was not a typical Western, where white Americans were indisputable heroes. Brian Rouleau, in *Empire's Nursery*, argues that Westerns were 'a key vehicle through which racialist and white supremacist ideology was presented to many young Americans' (30) and that 'it was rare, after all, for Indians to appear in this literature as anything other than miscreants motivated by bloodlust' (26). Prebble depicts four different groups of people, European-Americans, African-Americans, Mexicans, and Indians, in conflict and in uneasy alliance with each other in nineteenth-century Oklahoma. Although focalised through the white lieutenant in charge of a company of African-American soldiers, Prebble makes clear the feelings and opinions of other characters through gestures, facial expressions, and dialogue. These characters often remain silent in Lieutenant Byrne's company, a narrative technique that constantly reminds readers of the uneven distribution of power, even in the 'freedom' of the Wild West.

Lieutenant Byrne is not a typical American officer. Irish-born, he emigrated after his family were run off their land by Englishmen. Byrne tells a white frontierswoman that the English 'wanted the land and we had to go. Like they clear the Indians out here' (69). Yet despite being evicted from his childhood home, Byrne's lasting memory of the event is 'the sight of a squadron of green-jacketed dragoons leaping a dry-stone wall in Galway ... that had filled him with admiration for the horse-soldier, and a terribly desperate desire to be one himself' (41). He says he 'had never really understood' (41) why he admired people who were forcing him from his home, but it is clearly their power he wants, power to command and power to be an enforcer rather than one of the powerless. His ambivalence about power, however, ensures that he achieves none of it. He resents being put in command of an African-American company rather than a white company, as it is seen as a second-rate command; yet he turns a blind eye when he is disobeyed by his soldiers and the Comanche because he understands their feelings of powerlessness. He speaks up (reluctantly) when white people refer to his soldiers or the Comanches by racial slurs; but although he tells his sergeant 'I don't give a damn about your colour' (8), he has to catch himself from using racial slurs.

It is his sergeant's disapproval that keeps Byrne from using racial slurs. Sergeant Salem is, like Upfield's detective, of dual heritage, the son of an African-American enslaved woman and her white enslaver. Salem is better educated than most of the company (including Byrne) because, as he says ironically, 'I had an enlightened owner, I was told' (9). He acts as Byrne's conscience throughout most of the story, as in this incident where Byrne tells one of the company to make coffee:

> 'I want coffee for Mr. Tatum and myself, and I want it as black as your. . .' He saw the quick clouding of Salem's eyes. 'You want something, sergeant?'
> 'Black as my damned hide, yes sir', said Crispin. 'Yes, *sir!*' . . .
> 'No', said Byrne, 'just black. What's your complaint, Sergeant Salem?'
> 'There's no complaint, lieutenant', said Salem in a gentle voice, and he saluted and turned away. (6)

Byrne responds to several of Salem's spoken and unspoken criticisms about treatment of African-Americans, but when Salem criticises his decisions about the Comanche, Byrne refuses to listen. Byrne persists in pursuing the Comanche despite the pursuit ending in the death of the Indians, a white child, several horses, and most of Byrne's own company.

Prebble's message, that the pursuit of power leads to widespread destruction, has a peculiarly racial dimension because Byrne has a good relationship with the Comanche leader, Quasia, until they kidnap a white child whose mother Byrne fancies. Anne Norvall is living on her own after her husband's death, and fears the Comanche people. Byrne tells her, 'They're hard to understand, but maybe we should try' (124). When she calls them 'animals' (124), Byrne continues to protest. But after Anne's brother shoots a Comanche coming to the house in peace, and Comanches accidentally kill Anne's daughter and kidnap her son, Byrne stops seeing them as humans and hunts them down like the animals that Anne considers them to be. Nonetheless, Serraillier's 'Notes and Corrections' on the book suggest that he felt 'the book deals with such topics as race relations and colour in an intelligent and sympathetic way'.

Early New Windmills published by Serraillier including Black or Brown characters are, like early Peacocks, set outside the United Kingdom. Even though both publishers clearly want to broaden the horizons of their readers through stories of other cultures, it is the wide world, rather than England, where 'others' can be found. Whereas Peacock tended to sidestep issues of racism and focus only on the consequences of cross-racial interaction for white characters, Serraillier's choices for New Windmill show a consideration of the effects of colonisation and racism on people of colour as well. It is perhaps unsurprising that New Windmills with Black *British* characters appeared much sooner than they did in Peacocks.

Stepping Out or Out of Step? New Windmill and Black Britain

In the late 1960s, New Windmill began acknowledging that Britain's population (especially the school-aged population) was changing; the total estimated population of people of colour in Britain in 1966 was nearly one million, about a third of whom were under the age of fifteen (Rose 99). Despite Serraillier's commitment to reaching a wide variety of readers in schools, the literature he chose continued to be focused on and focalised through white middle-class characters, even when they included Black characters in Britain. Often, Black characters were either new to Britain or only temporary visitors or both. Nonetheless, the books that Serraillier chose showed Britain's young white population to be accepting of and interested in Black people, and keen to forge friendships across racial lines, sometimes against their parents' wishes and sometimes putting themselves in danger to maintain these friendships.

A good example of this is one of the earliest books that Serraillier published involving Black people in contemporary Britain, Nina Bawden's *On the Run* (Victor Gollancz 1964; New Windmills 1967). *On the Run* was one of Bawden's first novels for children, written following a trip to Kenya (Tucker, 'Nina Bawden'), significant because the Black child character in the story is not British but African. Bawden's protagonist is the son of a prime minister imprisoned while the British decide whether to extradite him. 'Until two months ago, Chief Okapi had been the Prime Minister of Tiga. Tiga was a rich country in East Africa, roughly the same size as Kenya, but much richer because there were diamond mines in the high mountains of the North' (31). Okapi's son, Thomas, is being kept in a nondescript house to protect him from his Uncle Joseph, who is involved in the coup of Okapi's government. Ben, the white British boy living next door, saves Thomas by running away with him to Ben's aunt's house in the (also imaginary) seaside town of Henstable.

Bawden's Tiga, possibly based on the northern Ethiopian region of Tigray, is a collection of British colonialist ideas about Africa formed and solidified during Empire. With its diamond mines (a feature of British Empire children's books, perhaps most notably in H. Rider Haggard's *King Solomon's Mines* and Frances Hodgson Burnett's *A Little Princess*), lions (34), and missionaries (35), Tiga could be a representation of pre-independence Africa if it were not for the military coup. While lions and missionaries serve to indicate Tiga's/Africa's lack of (and need for) white civilisation, the military coup confirms it. Ben asks why an African prime minister would be imprisoned in England, and his father responds:

> In England, when politicians disagree, they have a General
> Election, and the party that gets the most votes, wins. But in
> some places things aren't so – so tidy. Sometimes the people in
> power decide to imprison the people who were in power before
> they were, so they can't oppose them any more. (29–30)

African countries have 'untidy' governments now that they are independent, and Britain and America must step in to help them become more civilised.

Thomas does not face any overt prejudice in Bawden's novel; however, Bawden carefully 'others' him from the start. When Ben first meets Thomas, he speaks to him in Swahili, a habit from Ben's childhood spent in Kenya. 'Ben had spoken in Swahili *because the boy was African*' (18; emphasis mine). Thomas had not yet spoken, and there is nothing to indicate this African origin except his appearance: 'He had a dark face with a purple sheen on it like a ripe plum and thick, black, woolly hair' (18). Labelling the boy as African before he speaks and without any clear evidence other than his appearance is problematic. It allows Ben, and the reader, to see Black people as not belonging in England. And yet, at the time when Bawden wrote *On the Run*, this is plainly not true – even in the world of her book. Thomas and Ben see children playing on a bombsite, and Thomas notes that he is not conspicuous:'There are a lot of boys here who are dark-skinned, like me' (108). Bawden's novel both recognises and denies the presence of Black people as a permanent part of Britain.

Two years after publishing *On the Run*, Serraillier published a book that more directly confronted racial relations in Britain, Josephine Kamm's *Out of Step* (Brockhampton Press 1962; New Windmill 1969). Kamm, wife of publisher George Kamm, became one of the first British authors to write contemporary YA problem novels. *Out of Step* focuses on cross-racial relationships and racial prejudice in Britain. The book opens by clearly contrasting the way sixteen-year-old white working-class Betty sees Bob Francis, a photography student from British Guiana, and how racist thugs see him. 'As he came towards her she saw that he was tall and slight, with black, close-cropped hair and a golden-brown skin . . . He looks nice, Betty thought' (7). But before she can speak to him, 'a crowd of men and boys stream around the corner' (8). They call Bob a 'black monkey' (8) and tell him to go 'back to the jungle' (8). Betty lives in a divided Britain – those who think 'the Government ought to send the blacks back to their own country, and then things'd settle down here' (20), as Betty's mother believes, and those who know that 'they *are* British, same as us' (20), as Betty's father believes.

The novel acts as an anti-racist teaching tool. Kamm indicates that all white people, however politically inclined, have to learn about Black people in their country. Betty is constantly being corrected or taught throughout the novel; the Irish neighbour describes Caribbean foods from the market (30); an African woman tells her about hair straightening (63); and Bob explains about colourism in Caribbean communities (104). Kamm emphasises seeing people as individuals by having Bob explain to Betty that he would not run with a rowdy crowd, just because they were West Indian (64); and by having Betty's dad tell her brother Brian that the concept of 'keeping the English race pure' (77) was a falsity. Overall, Kamm's focalisation of the action through Betty allows readers to grow and learn along with her. Ian Serraillier's wife Anne Serraillier, who shepherded the book to publication along with Hilary Birley, felt that the book had a significant role to play for white working-class readers. Writing to Birley, she commented, 'It will certainly appeal to "reluctant readers", as the simple direct style makes no great intellectual demands on the reader, whilst it skilfully engages attention and sympathy and makes a strong plea for tolerance and understanding' ('Letter to Hilary Birley'). Tolerance and understanding are critical for white working-class readers so they turn out more like Betty and less like her brother.

Kamm rarely ended her novels happily. *Out of Step* concludes with uncertainty; as I write in *Children's Publishing and Black Britain*, 'Betty's parents may disagree in some ways, but they agree that Betty's hopes of marrying Bob are doomed' (21). Betty, however, does not give up. Even though Bob refuses to commit to Betty until she is twenty-one, she is determined to wait. 'She realized . . . that if he could endure the hurt and the waiting, then so must she; and she saw that in the long run the hurt might even be worse for him than for her' (184). Betty's greater concern for Bob's feelings than for her own, argues Kamm, is what makes her mature enough to love another person – offering hope, but not certainty, that their love affair may carry on. Nonetheless, it is Betty's romance that readers are ultimately directed to care about, not Bob's life and experiences in Britain.

Maybe Multicultural: Non-Fiction New Windmills

As with Peacock, New Windmill published occasional non-fiction. Most non-fiction published by Serraillier was biography or autobiography. Eleanor Doorly's scientific biographies, Martin Lindsay's *The Epic of Captain Scott* (Peter Davies 1933; New Windmills 1966) and Charlie Chaplin's autobiography, *My Early Years* (Chivers and New Windmills 1964) were all part of the New Windmill catalogue.

Serraillier also (before Kaye Webb) published J. H. Williams' *Elephant Bill* (Penguin 1956; New Windmill 1957). This choice is significant, because while Williams' book is a problematic adventure story in terms of its attitude towards Indigenous people, it is also a conservation story, as Williams attempted to get elephants to safety during wartime (unlike Jim Corbett's *Man-Eaters of Kumaon*). Serraillier often published books with a conservationist message, and in so doing put conservation above depicting racial relations in a positive or accurate way. *Sajo and her Beaver People* (1967), for example, is a story about the cruelty of beaver trapping, and the original publication led to half a million people attending lectures by the author. The author listed on the New Windmill edition of *Sajo* is Grey Owl, as it had been when the book was originally published by Lovat Dickson and Thompson in 1935. However, in 1938, just a year after the author died – 'Grey Owl' was unmasked by his own English aunts as Archibald Belaney, who had been born in Sussex and had no tribal affiliation at all. The *Hull Daily Mail*, who in 1936 had praised the author as 'a Modern Hiawatha' ('The Red Man is Happy Again' 5), in 1938 published a front page article calling him 'a fake who had piled up a fortune at the expense of a credulous public' ('Did Grey Owl 'Spoof' Hull Public?' 1). In short, Serraillier should have known that Grey Owl was born Archibald Belaney, yet he chose to leave the 'Indian' name on the book, allowing the misrepresentation of Belaney as a tribal member, and romanticising 'native' ways.

Romanticising 'native' ways is also a feature of one of the only 'career' books that Serraillier ever published. Rachel Scott's *A Wedding Man Is Nicer Than Cats, Miss* (David and Charles 1971; New Windmill 1974) is a curious choice for New Windmill, as it describes the two years that Scott spent teaching in an all-immigrant school in Yorkshire. The Serrailliers felt the book had value beyond suggesting a career in teaching. Ian Serraillier argues in his reader report that as well as future teachers, 'other readers too are going to find a great deal of interest in the study of relationships that the book reveals' ('Readers Report *Wedding Man*'). Although focusing on new British citizens from India and Pakistan, it shows their lives through the eyes of a white teacher. Scott describes their customs with sympathy, but not empathy, and often pities her students and their families when they do things differently to British custom. For example, when an Islamic leader comes to town, Scott and her fellow teacher are invited to meet him. Scott comments that she 'had enjoyed the festive occasion and had been made aware, as so often before, of the variety of life in a multi-racial town' (149); yet when she sees the Islamic leader's wife in a niqab, she compares it to 'a shroud' (149) and 'shuddered in the July sunshine. . . . The impact of that hooded figure was startling, even painful' (149). Scott never explains *why* the vision is so painful to her, but presumably she worries that the leader's wife is unhappy in traditional dress. However, as she never speaks to the leader's wife, she is making assumptions based only on her own cultural expectations.

Indeed, if there is any message to *A Wedding Man*, it is that new British Indian and Pakistani students must learn, not just the English language, but to conform to English expectations as well. Throughout the book, Scott discusses teaching children to be 'proud of being Indian or Pakistani' (35) while at the same time asking them to 'conform to such western standards of behaviour as would enable them to take their place in the community without embarrassment to themselves' (36). Indian and Pakistani customs and habits are described as 'sickly and distasteful' (36), 'disconcerting' (37), 'uncivilised' (44), and causing 'revulsion' (187); Scott is sympathetic to cultural differences but still argues that 'customs which conflicted with accepted practice, or with the day to day running of a school, had therefore to be tempered, perhaps eliminated' (35). And the onus is on the children to accept assimilation and silently turn the other cheek to racism. Even though Scott tells the children they are likely to face prejudice, she 'begged them not to listen to the name-calling, not to retaliate, and to remember that the people who were most hostile were those who knew nothing about them' (186). Scott goes on to try to 'eliminate' those things that make the British Indian and Pakistani communities different, and to encourage her students to follow suit, discussing 'some Asian customs which would certainly invite criticism' (187) such as male friends holding hands. Scott's book was written before, but published in New Windmill after, the expulsion of Asians from Uganda in 1972. Becky Taylor notes that anti-immigrant hostility in the country was high prior to and after the expulsion, and 'when the British government caved in to internal and international pressures to take responsibility for Ugandan Asians with UK passports, it did so in a highly charged atmosphere in which hostility for the expellees was expressed politically, in the media and on the street' (122). For any Black or Asian teens reading Scott's book amid such hostility, her message to turn the other cheek may have seemed extremely naive.

Serraillier's New Windmills make an attempt to address new immigrant populations who, by the late 1960s, were changing the face of British schools. But the 'multicultural' literature that he chose always depicted cultures (both in and out of Britain) from a white British perspective. Much like fiction Serraillier published around the same time, non-fiction focused on the education of and benefit to white British readers. While there was, throughout these books, an effort to teach readers and characters anti-racist principles, Black British and British Asian characters, as well as those characters of colour from outside Britain, had to shoulder the burden of either explaining their customs or eradicating them for the comfort of white readers and characters. Perhaps unsurprisingly, these books are all written by white authors; it is not until Serraillier begins publishing authors from Black and Asian communities both in and out of Britain that British readers are offered literature that is sympathetic to readers of colour.

Opening up the Classroom to Sir, with Love: New Windmills by Black Writers

Ian Serraillier was fortunate in having access to two adult series published by Heinemann, the African Writers Series established in 1958 (its first publication was Chinua Achebe's *Things Fall Apart*) and Caribbean Writers Series established in 1970 with Michael Anthony's *The Year in San Fernando*. These two series became an important outlet for writers in the former British Empire to publish in English and have books distributed globally. Serraillier's earliest inclusion of work by Black writers for New Windmill were Achebe's and Anthony's books. However, although they were listed in the back of New Windmills, it is unclear whether specific New Windmill editions were ever produced or whether they remained as part of the African and Caribbean writers' series, and were simply suggested for classrooms through New Windmill. All three series were part of the Heinemann Educational Books division, and so could be easily packaged together.

However, in 1971 Serraillier published a story with a Black British character written by a Black British author. E. R. Braithwaite's *To Sir, with Love* was originally published in 1959 by Bodley Head, three years before Josephine Kamm's *Out of Step*, but it was not until two years after publishing Kamm's book that Serraillier added the semi-autobiographical story of British-Guianese author Braithwaite's experiences teaching in London's East End. Indeed, the book had been considered – and rejected – by New Windmills in 1964 (Serraillier, 'Notes and Corrections'), and again in 1967 when a schoolteacher wrote to New Windmills to recommend it. Hilary Birley told the teacher that the Serrailliers 'did not feel confident' about the book. Anne Serraillier commented to Tony Beal that although it might make 'good follow-up reading' to Kamm's *Out of Step*, she felt it had too many 'obvious flaws' ('Letter to Tony Beal'). The Serrailliers only found confidence in it after it had been made into a successful film starring Sidney Poitier. Serraillier often published books that had been made into films. These included Rumer Godden's *Black Narcissus* (Peter Davies 1939; New Windmills 1963), set in India, made into a film in 1947. It was a way to get teenagers, who spent more money on movies than on books, to read for pleasure. Braithwaite's novel, set in urban contemporary London in one of the big comprehensive schools seen as dumping grounds for problem students, provided Serraillier with an opportunity to reach readers with similar backgrounds.

Like Nina Bawden's *On the Run* and Josephine Kamm's *Out of Step*, the main Black character of Braithwaite's book, Rick Braithwaite, is educated and middle-class. However, because the book has a Black author writing a Black character, *To Sir, with Love* is about Rick's experience of racism instead of white characters' understanding of it. While *Out of Step* focuses on the romantic relationship between Bob and Betty, and only peripherally notes Bob's outside life, *To Sir* confronts racism on the street, in classrooms, at work, and in relationships. Braithwaite did not write the book for teenagers, as Kamm did; perhaps this accounts for its direct, realistic, and often angry depiction of racism.

Braithwaite's account, like Kamm's, aims to teach white British readers about their former empire. Early in *Out of Step*, Bob tells a group of gathered white people, 'I'm not a foreigner... I'm British' (15). He goes on to say 'proudly' (15) that 'England is my mother-country' (15), despite just having been chased down by racist white British men and boys. Bob's attitude throughout the novel is one of pride in England. Rick Braithwaite's relationship to England is far more complicated; as he says, 'it is wonderful to be British – until one comes to Britain' (38). Braithwaite spends much of the novel's first fifty pages looking for work in London and facing rejection after rejection; he reflects bitterly that 'my black skin . . . had not mattered when I volunteered for aircrew service in 1940' (36). But despite his service and a university degree, he is not welcome anywhere but the East End slums, 'a tough area' (46) with 'tawdry, jaded' girls (49) and 'scruffier, coarser, dirtier' boys (49) where it is Braithwaite's task to keep order rather than teach.

Like Kamm's book, Braithwaite's includes a narrative arc about transforming white racists into tolerant people. In *Out of Step*, Betty's brother Brian is a member of a gang called the Pure-Blooded Englishmen who attack the West Indian Club where Bob takes Betty on a date. Bob saves Brian from being beaten up, as well as from getting arrested. Although Brian at first acts sullen, he soon agrees to leave the gang. 'He had left it not only under pressure from his father or even because he saw how wrong it was, but also because he admired the courage and leadership which Bob Francis had shown' (87), Kamm writes. It is up to individual Black people to represent their community well, so white people will lose their prejudices. Although the focus is on Brian's conversion through Bob's actions, Bob shows concern for Black people as well. When two fellow West Indians at the club pull out knives in response to the racist attack, Bob suggests they back down 'unless you want *us* to get into trouble with the police' (69). They comply, but are still 'bound over' (76) on felony charges, along with the gang leaders. No more is said about their case; the story moves quickly on to Brian's conversion.

Braithwaite's story also includes a conversion that rests on the Black character to bring it about. Rick's students are casually prejudiced; they are surprised when his blood is red (105), and ask questions about whether he washes, feels the cold, or cuts his hair (106); Rick purports not to mind their questions. In a geography lesson, when one student suggests that South Africans are white and 'natives' are black, Rick patiently responds, 'No, Fernman. You're a native of London and so is Seales, but you are of different colours. I am a native of British Guiana, and there are thousands of British Guianese who are white-skinned and blonde, red-headed or brunette' (98). Rick generally responds to his students and other white people with patience, silence, or amusement rather than anger.

But Rick's patience with white people does not always work. He dates a white teacher, Gillian, who gets angry when he remains silent about bad treatment in a restaurant. Indeed, she blames him for not making 'a big, bloody awful scene' (141) because, as she says, 'Someone else always has to fight for you, to take your part. Clinty stood up for you against Weston; the Dare girl stood up for you on the train; was I supposed to stand up for you tonight?' (142). Gillian does not see it as her responsibility to speak out against racism (as Betty does in *Out of Step*); she thinks that, as a grown-up, Rick should take responsibility for himself. Gillian does not understand the structural racism and constant micro-aggressions that Rick experiences every day, and she is ready to break off their relationship until he explains 'about my life in Britain, the whole thing, everything' (144). They decide to stay together, and Rick even meets Gillian's parents, but her parents offer 'the same old excuses, the same old arguments, hitting below the belt' (173) about dual heritage children being 'unwanted' (173). Her father insists that they wait 'six months at least, before taking any further action' (174). Gillian acquiesces; she does not seem to see her father's request for patience as problematic or his arguments as reinforcing racial hierarchies as Betty did in *Out of Step*. Braithwaite's novel asks white people to see their actions as cowardly and victim-blaming, and suggests everyone must take part in the removal of racism. But the Serrailliers hesitated about this book, preferring Kamm's, with its Black British character, which (as Anne Serraillier said) 'makes a plea for tolerance' from white readers, and Scott's, which had encouraged assimilation as the best route for people of colour.

After 1980, Serraillier (like Webb and Chambers) stepped back from New Windmill. Although the imprint continued to publish books with Black or Asian characters, many were written by white authors, including Geraldine Kaye's *Comfort Herself* (Methuen 1984; New Windmill 1987) and Nina Bawden's *The Robbers* (Victor Gollancz 1979; New Windmill 1981). *To Sir, with Love* was one of only a handful of books that Serraillier published in New Windmill by a Black British or British Asian author. Ultimately, Serraillier was cautious about what he did and did not publish, particularly when it came to issues of diversity. It was important to him, especially as time went on, that books (or at least their authors) had proven track records with both students and teachers – and primarily with teachers.

Serraillier offered a more diverse vision of Britain before 1980 than that found in Peacock, but it was still largely through middle-class, white-authored viewpoints. These viewpoints were also dominant in the primary market for New Windmill, classroom and school libraries.

One of the authors that Serraillier chose not to publish, even though her work was published in two other Heinemann series (their short-lived YA imprint, Pyramids, and a reluctant readers series) was Joan Tate. However, Tate *was* published by Macmillan Topliners' editor Aidan Chambers. The brief examination of her work that follows indicates key differences between the two publishers.

Crossover Author: Joan Tate, Heinemann, and Topliners

Ian Serraillier's New Windmill series was designed to take children beyond the classics. An article in the *Guardian* suggested: 'When Ian Serraillier was teaching back in the late forties, children were only given the classics to read at school. Contemporary novelists were considered adult fare, not suitable for children' ('Fiction of Their Time' 14). Compared with Webb's Peacock imprint, Serraillier's New Windmills certainly offered a wider range of experiences in books 'to encourage further reading' ('Ian Serraillier' A17), as Tony Beal points out. But Beal's phrase suggests that students not only had the books, but read them; it was another Heinemann author and editor, Joan Tate, who encouraged non-readers. Tate told Chambers, 'My own books came from repeated remarks that there were no books for the young who *didn't* read, rather than couldn't' (*Reluctant Reader* 94). Tate was best-known for her translation of Nordic writers, including Ingmar Bergman; her *Guardian* obituary, written by Laurie Thompson and Cleodie Mackinnon, does not even mention her writing for young people (24). But in the mid-1960s, Heinemann gave Tate her own imprint, the Joan Tate Books; later, several of these were published in Heinemann's Pyramid imprint for young adults.

Both the Joan Tate Books and Pyramids were specifically designed 'for the "reluctant" teenager' (St John 562), a group vastly underserved by both Peacock and New Windmill. Kaye Webb had little interest in reluctant readers; the Serrailliers occasionally discussed this group in their notes, but primarily focused on white working-class reluctant readers when they addressed them at all. Elaine Moss, in 'Reluctant at Fifteen', argues that for this group of readers 'the classics are too difficult, many modern novels too advanced in technique, the story in the teenage weekly too synthetic to fulfil any real function. They need books which are basically adult and serious . . . and which tell a story vividly, briefly and in some depth' (23). Sheila Ray, a librarian who advocated for the availability of books for all types of readers, suggested that Tate was an excellent author for reluctant readers, 'writing fluently and readably' (185) in books such as the Pyramid-published *Out of the Sun* (1968), about a seventeen-year-old Black girl from Grenada who lives with her family in London.

Out of the Sun was actually a reprint of two books from her Joan Tate Books series in a single volume, *Jenny* (1964) and *Mrs Jenny* (1966). It is useful to think about how the Joan Tate Books were different from New Windmills. The Joan Tate Books were illustrated throughout, often by top-quality illustrators; *Jenny* and *Mrs Jenny*, for example, were illustrated by white illustrator Charles Keeping, who would go on to win the Kate Greenaway Medal in 1967 for *Charley, Charlotte and the Golden Canary*, the first Kate Greenaway winner to have a Black central character. New Windmills were also often illustrated, though not as prolifically as the Joan Tate Books, which each have more than a dozen illustrations in stories of less than sixty pages. New Windmills were hardbacks, part of Serraillier's push to get contemporary fiction treated seriously in schools; the Joan Tate Books, which were also sent to schools, were paperbacks to appeal to reluctant readers. The Joan Tate Books were contemporary stories, with predominantly working-class characters. This is where Tate's books about Black Britons differ from the books in New Windmill; in the few cases where a Black character is included in a contemporary New Windmill novel, they are educated and/or middle- or upper-class characters, even when the books are set in working-class Britain. Bob, in Josephine Kamm's *Out of Step*, Rick Braithwaite in *To Sir, with Love*, and Thomas in Bawden's *On the Run* all are either wealthier (Thomas) or better educated (Bob and Rick) than many white people who live in their London neighbourhoods.

Tate's Jenny, however, comes from a working-class household, with everyone living 'in the two rooms downstairs. There were only four of them so they were all very lucky really. Many of the coloured people in Wandchester had only one room for whole families' (*Jenny* 3). Jenny works in a supermarket, having left school at fifteen. Her best friend, a British Pakistani girl named Jindra, is the only significant character who is not Black British. White characters appear on the fringes, but Jenny does not mix much with them. She and Jindra work together, 'and they liked to be together [at work]. It was not that the other girls were rude or hostile to them. They were very friendly in their off-hand way. But somehow Jenny and Jindra felt safer together' (7). At sixteen, Jenny is chased by white 'hooligans' (19) who beat up several Black people in her area. A year later, she goes to a dance and is called a 'black tart' (38) when she dances with a white boy; other white boys threaten violence. Even though her father tells her, 'They're not all like that' (26), Jenny follows the counsel of her mother who tells her to 'stick to the coloured boys' (39). Like Josephine Kamm's *Out of Step*, Tate's *Jenny* explores cross-racial relationships; but unlike Kamm's Betty, Tate's Jenny cannot ignore the threat of racial violence that hangs over such a relationship. Unlike Kamm's Bob, Jenny sees her home as being Britain, where her family is now settled. Leaving for Grenada is not an option for her, as leaving for Guyana is for Bob. Jenny eventually marries a Black neighbour, Tim Gordon, from British Guiana.

And it is through Tim, indirectly, that Jenny finally reconciles with white Britons. After her marriage, Jenny goes to work in a care home; when one of the residents becomes ill, Jenny and Tim go to visit her in hospital. Miss Timmis asks Tim if he is from British Guiana, and when he says he is, the elderly woman tells him that she could tell because 'Many years ago when I was a girl, I used to teach in Cardiff . . . Some of my children were very like you. But of course they had been born in Cardiff. But their grandparents had come from Guiana' (*Mrs Jenny* 45). It turns out that this is not Miss Timmis' only connection with the West Indies. Upon her death, she leaves Jenny a box of her possessions, and in the box is a photograph of Miss Timmis' christening – which took place in the same town where Jenny was born in Grenada. Miss Timmis' parents were missionaries there. Unusually, Tate charts the long history of traffic between Britain and its (former) colonies, and suggests that only through understanding of and participation in this history will white and Black British people be able to get along successfully.

Like New Windmill, the Joan Tate Books were part of Heinemann's educational arm, but the audience was different. The paperback series was an experiment for Heinemann; when Tate's books were published in the company's trade YA imprint, Pyramids, they were published in hardback. This was a financial move on Heinemann's part, to ensure that the Pyramids 'were taken very largely by the public libraries, which indeed in those days absorbed some ninety per cent of the children's list' (St John 561–2). Most of Heinemann's books for young people were published in hardback first; Pan, the Heinemann paperback division, did not publish for young people at the time.

Many teenage readers saw hardback books as unappealing, however. Chambers, who was developing an editorial imprint for young adults, wanted to ensure that his books would be read. He approached Tate, who helped him put his ideas into a proposal for Heinemann. Tony Beal, then managing director for Heinemann Education, told Chambers he liked the idea, but 'we're not a commercial trade paperback imprint' (Pearson 180). Heinemann could only promise educational editions in paperback – along the lines of the Joan Tate books. Chambers responded, 'I don't mind having educational editions but we have to have commercial ones as well, otherwise to the kids this is not grown-up publishing, it's school stuff' (180). When Heinemann said it was impossible, Chambers took his idea to Macmillan, and Chambers' Topliners series was born.

Joan Tate remained friendly with Chambers and contributed several titles to Topliners, but never published anything for the imprint with Black protagonists, and indeed, only *Jenny* and *Mrs Jenny* ever did. The fact that her Black character's experiences of the terror of racism and the difficulties of connecting with white Britons were only considered good enough for Heinemann's series for reluctant readers and not New Windmill suggests that Serraillier thought his white middle-class readership would not understand or empathise with the story of a working-class Black girl. The fact that Chambers published Tate's books showcasing white fears and prejudices rather than books like *Jenny* calls into question how progressive Chambers' Topliners project was, at least in terms of issues of race.

3 Is It Always Like This? Topliners and Publishing for the Reluctant Reader of Colour

'But the first thing everybody says to him is – you're black.' *(Pope 49)*

In 1966, Aidan Chambers had been teaching for nine years in a secondary school. During this time, he found that a group of his students were naturally inclined to read – and another group were not. 'There were many who, although capable, read very few "literary" books for pleasure, and were never likely to' ('Topliners Press Release'). It is these readers, who Chambers labelled 'reluctant', that he hoped to serve in his YA imprint for Macmillan, Topliners, which launched in 1968.

Chambers was so convinced that reluctant readers needed special attention that he approached both Heinemann and Penguin with the idea to publish under a new or existing imprint. When he approached Heinemann, they initially responded favourably but would not publish books exclusively in paperback rather than in tandem with hardcover library or school editions, because the profit margins were so small. Chambers also discussed the idea with Kaye Webb in 1968. Peacocks, unlike New Windmills or other Heinemann imprints, were issued as paperbacks only, but Chambers felt that they could be more successful by appealing to a wider section of the reading population. He urged Webb to go in a new direction, one that used their most successful title, Beverley Cleary's *Fifteen*, as a model.

Chambers argued that *Fifteen* was a success in part because of its packaging, not only in paperback format but in its choice of a photographic cover. This appealed to teenagers who might not otherwise read: 'The unbookish would not accept Peacocks because the selection was wrong and the presentation that of children's books rather than adolescent books' (*Reluctant Reader* 138), he wrote. But Pearson suggests that Webb 'met Chambers' attempts to pursue his vision of a new kind of teenage publishing within Penguin with little enthusiasm' (125) and decided against appointing Chambers as a Peacock editor. Chambers' failure to convince Peacock and New Windmill of the efficacy of his ideas only strengthened his resolve to produce literature that could bring new readers into the world of books. However, Chambers maintained his admiration for Webb's sales techniques, and suggested several as boosts for Topliners, including a newsletter sent out to readers, something akin to '<u>Puffin Post</u>, the archetypal publicity vehicle for Puffin books. It is so very good – and so very effective – because it employs the traditionally popular form of reading children like' (Chambers, 'Proposal for a TOPLINERS magazine'). Chambers also suggested a slogan such as, 'Tuck into a Topliner' ('Letter to Martin Pick', 4 May 1975) that echoed Webb's 'Pick a Puffin' from the previous decade.

Of all the imprints in this study, Topliners is the shortest-lived. Peacock lasted from the early 1960s until around 1980 when it was subsumed into Puffin Plus (but many of the titles continued to be printed for young adults under this new name); Heinemann's New Windmill still publish new titles, although under different editorship. Macmillan Topliners, however, lasted about as long as Macmillan's other experimental imprint, Leila Berg's working-class reading series, Nippers – which is to say until the late 1970s (Chambers retired as general editor in 1979, and the imprint did not last long after that). The imprints had much in common. Both were concerned with reaching young people who did not feel comfortable in the world of books, because books did not reflect them or their everyday realities. Both focused initially on white (and primarily working-class) readers, only turning to Black and Asian readers later. And both were keen to publish books with 'real' rather than 'literary' language.

Neither Berg nor Chambers had direct models for their series, but Macmillan Education's commissioning editor, Michael Wace, believed that working-class and reluctant readers needed to find themselves in books as easily as middle-class readers did. Chambers had already sought advice from Joan Tate, a prolific translator and author of a Heinemann Educational series of books for older but non-proficient readers. Tate had urged Chambers to stand firm when Heinemann refused to originate books in paperbacks. She agreed with him that books such as hers were necessary, not just in the classroom but in bookstores and stationers as well. Tate gave Chambers a manuscript to start Topliners off – the book, *Sam and Me* would become Topliners biggest all-time seller – and other authors followed. But while characters in early Topliners did depict lives typically ignored by Peacock and even New Windmill, such as young people in foster care or married teenagers, the main focus was initially on white reluctant readers.

The Outsiders, in and out of Books: Early Topliners

Chambers' desire to address reluctant readers came in part from his own experience. He came from the 'unliterary working class' ('Letter from England' 80), and 'became a reader when I found myself, my own culture, my own kind, my own way of living in fiction' (Pearson 184). Many of the books he preferred as a teenager were American, and he found that British teenagers in the 1960s did also. Chambers, in *Booktalk*, argued that 'the reason that I and many other English readers . . . find themselves at home in American literature is that it doesn't begin by alienating, but by opening itself to the reader' ('Letter from England' 82) regardless of social class. Books like Paul Zindel's *I Never Loved Your Mind*, Robert Cormier's *The Chocolate War*, and S. E. Hinton's *The Outsiders* were all popular with British teenagers despite very American references.

It is unsurprising, therefore, that one of the earliest titles Chambers produced was an American reprint, Robert Lipsyte's *The Contender* (Harper & Row 1967, Topliners 1969). This title exemplifies the kind of writing that Chambers valued; it put readers in the mind of the main character, Alfred, before the end of the first paragraph. 'He waited on the stoop until twilight, pretending to watch the sun melt into the dirty grey Harlem sky. . . . Another five minutes, he thought. I'll give Jones another five minutes' (7). The narrative slide from omniscient to first person, common to American teen fiction, was new to British readers in 1969 and would be one of the traits that Chambers looked for in selecting Topliners manuscripts.

Chambers called *The Contender* 'a tense and exciting story about life as it is . . . seen the way today's generation sees it' on the front-cover blurb. For most British teenagers, Lipsyte's novel included everything the media had warned them about America: drugs, gangs, poverty, racism, and violence. In fact, Alfred escapes from gangs only by joining a boxing club, where he is eventually beaten badly by a white boxer. He survives to rescue his drug-addicted friend from bleeding to death from a knife wound, and the book ends with the two injured African-American teenagers, clinging to each other in a world that has mostly rejected them. Given this vision of American teenagers, it is instructive to consider how Topliners viewed Black British characters at this same time. Three early titles show Chambers' vision for the series in terms of accessibility, appeal, and language; but equally, these three books showcase the problems that white British publishers and authors, even progressive and well-meaning ones, had in depicting and attracting readers of colour.

The first of these books, *Clipper* (1969), was written by Joan Tate as a sequel to another Topliner, *Whizz Kid* (1969). The books portray a relationship between white teenagers Clee and Nibs, who live in an unnamed town north of London and south of Lancashire, an area rarely depicted in books for young people (which primarily included characters from either London or the rural countryside). Clee is considered a slow learner, but Nibs calls her 'Whizz Kid'. In describing herself in *Clipper*, Clee writes, 'I can't imagine how my mind works. No one had ever suggested that I even had one, before I met Nibs' (12). Clee's character is very different from typical female heroines in Peacock or New Windmill novels, and is the very sort of character (and reader) that Chambers felt had been ignored – urban but not London-based, unsuccessful at school, more interested in relationships than career or education. In *Clipper*, the still-teenaged Clee marries Nibs and they have a baby (Clipper). Nibs' job takes the family to London, and they encounter a 'crazy collection of neighbours' (back cover blurb) that includes British Pakistanis and Black British people.

Upon learning of her new neighbours, Clee comments, 'There were a few black men at home, but not many. I'd never spoken to any of them' (56). She lumps the two Pakistanis together with Moses, the Afro-Caribbean man, calling them all 'darkies' (72). She finds them 'unfriendly . . . As if they didn't like us being here' (76). It never occurs to her that they might see her as the outsider; she, being white and British-born, believes she belongs by right to all of Britain. Although she concedes that 'I would have to do a bit of learning to live with other people' (56), Clee mistrusts her neighbours. She fears for her baby's safety in their company and continues to refer to them as 'darkies' (80) even after Nibs tells her to stop. Jessica Yates notes that references to 'darkies' are removed in the 1976 edition, but adds that 'the difficulty is that the nervous assumptions Clee makes about black people, which are to be proved wrong, are in themselves racist' ('Censorship in Children's Paperbacks' 186). Pearson notes that *Clipper* 'is a realistic portrayal of the assumptions and reactions of a young 1960s couple with no experience of people of colour' (145) but also that 'realistic portrayals of racism ran the risk of perpetuating racist attitudes' (145). Joan Tate, who had so successfully depicted Afro-Caribbean family life in her earlier books *Jenny* and *Mrs Jenny*, did not attempt to give the same depth to people of colour in books she published with Topliners. Her books for Topliners suggest that Chambers was more interested, at least early on, in addressing a white British audience, who would have formed the bulk of Topliners customers.

Changing populations in Britain (and more particularly London) continued to prompt Chambers to depict more diversity in Topliners, and Ray Pope's *Is It Always Like This?* (1970), which appeared a year after Tate's *Clipper*, was the first teenage novel to depict a British Asian on its photographic cover. 'Pakistani Tormon', as the inside front cover blurb refers to him, is not the central character (the book's cover does not actually depict the central character, gang leader Pinky). Tormon is shown holding a small white girl while an older white girl looks on; all three are smiling. This is a remarkably progressive cover; few young people's book covers at the time included people of colour. The ones that did often showed them as the object of white readers' and characters' curious and sometimes fearful gazes. The New Windmill edition of John Prebble's *The Buffalo Soldiers*, for example, is dominated by a white figure holding a gun while staring at a tiny figure of a Comanche off in the distance. Rumer Godden's *The Peacock Spring*, in the Peacock edition, has a white girl, dressed in white and unsmiling, staring up at a mostly naked Indian with downcast eyes. Tormon, by contrast, is gazing at the reader, smiling, while the little white girl gazes at him adoringly. This underscores Chambers' desire to use photographic realism to appeal to readers of colour and suggest they belong in books.

However, the depiction of this happy group under the book's title – *Is It Always Like This?* – in bold blue letters would immediately, in 1970, evoke the response: not by a long chalk. The contrast between the united 'family' group on Pope's cover and Clee's hysterical reaction to her British Pakistani neighbours in *Clipper* just a year previously suggests that white reactions to communities of British Asians were not always so welcoming. And the text of Pope's novel underscores this doubt about 'new' British Asians.

Like Clee in Tate's book, white Britons lump Tormon together with other 'new immigrants' of colour. Although Pope acknowledges that Tormon is not Pakistani but 'English Pakistani' (8), the character is clearly marked out as different from white Britons. 'His dark face, lustrous eyes and straight black hair led the gang into occasional fights' (8). Some fights result from the racial epithet that Tormon is called by white Britons, which made 'Pinky angry' (8). Interestingly, Pinky gets angry because the name-caller has misnamed Tormon as Black, rather than Asian, although he argues that he would also 'bash' a white person who used a racial slur against Black people. Nonetheless, Pinky's awareness of racial hierarchies developed during the British Empire indicates that these attitudes were still very much in place in 1970s Britain. Pinky is not above using people's fear to his own advantage; he suggests that Tormon's 'dusky face with pearl-white teeth and lustrous eyes' (12) comes in handy to scare away tramps attempting to take over the railway archway where the gang has its headquarters. This is not imagery that would appeal to British Asian readers who, as Peter Fryer notes in *Staying Power* 'had been under attack from fascists and police ... forced to defend themselves, since nobody else could or would' (402). Pope's Pinky uses Tormon's appearance to benefit the rest of the (white) gang; Tormon's appearance certainly does not advantage Tormon himself.

Pope's novel repeats stereotypes of people of colour, often by using naïve characters to do so. The plot revolves around two abandoned white children adopted by Pinky's gang; when they first appear, the girl asks why Tormon has 'a dirty face and hands? ... Why doesn't he wash it off?' (28). Tormon responds with a biologically incorrect but familiar stereotype of his own; he says his skin 'got burned in the sun' because he is 'from a hotter country' (28). In this way, Pope has his character of colour 'othering' himself. Tormon accepts that white people do not want him around. When the gang entices a girl, Pat, to come look after the children, she criticises them, saying, 'You shouldn't leave that little girl with a coloured boy ... It isn't – it isn't – nice!' (47). Tormon responds by leaving. '"I will go", he said precisely, " – and – and then, perhaps, it will be nice"' (47). Pat's lashing out at Tormon's presence is an example of white fragility, defined by Robin Diangelo as 'a form of bullying; I am going to make it so miserable for you to confront me – no matter how diplomatically you try to do so – that you will simply back off, give up, and never raise the issue again' (112). Pat's fear requires people of colour – Tormon – to excuse her, rather than Pat accepting that her attitude is racist and she must work to change it.

Pat and Tormon's friendship develops as the book continues, but it relies on Tormon accepting white British customs and abandoning his own British Asian ones. Pope, like Rachel Scott, encourages British Asians to accommodate white British intolerance and even racism about their customs. Pat tries to link her arm through Tormon's; when he pulls away, she insists they hold hands, despite his request 'to understand me and not be offended' (75). In fact, Tormon avoids making white people feel uncomfortable throughout the book. He does not go looking for the children's parents with the rest of the gang: '"I should not find out anything. They will not talk to strangers." And he raised his black hand suggestively' (78). This comment and gesture prompts Pat to ask the title question, 'Is it always like this?' (79), to which Tormon responds, 'Sometimes it is worse' (79).

The final scene in which Tormon appears indicates again the problematic nature of white authors depicting people of colour. Tormon is in the gang's hideout when Pat 'burst in, seething with rage' (140) because a 'moron on the street corner' (140) has called her a racial epithet for being seen with Tormon. Tormon apologises to Pat, and suggests they not be seen together. Pat insists that she will not let anyone tell her what to do, but Tormon never gets to speak in the novel again, so readers do not know how he is feeling. Instead, readers are encouraged to think that white people's emotions and well-being matter most, and good people of colour will do their best to accommodate them, even at the expense of their own sense of self. Early Topliners were unique in depicting people of colour in contemporary Britain – but white authors who depicted them were more concerned with how these characters affected white characters (and, possibly, white readers) than with characters of colour.

In the same year that Pope's book was published, the *Times Educational Supplement* ran a contest for young writers between eleven and eighteen. Chambers subsequently published several entries in a Topliner entitled

I Want to Get Out (1971). As a former teacher, he had always had an interest in young people's voices, but by publishing their stories, Chambers was part of a trend. WH Smith and the *Daily Mirror* had been running a competition for young writers since 1959, and small community presses such as Centerprise in Hackney had published young writers, including Black and Asian teens, in the early 1970s with surprising success. Chambers was eager to publish teenagers' own 'understanding of life, what it means and is and might be' (*I Want to Get Out* front cover blurb).

Like other early Topliners, however, *I Want to Get Out* was an understanding of life from an exclusively white perspective, according to photographs of winners published in the *Times Educational Supplement* ('Story Competition' 14). Only two stories mention Black Britons at all. Faith Kendrick's 'Lunchbreak' is an impressionistic story of a girl, Kate, finding purpose in life while wandering through her school during her lunch period. One of the girls she sees is 'Lorena, a coloured girl she knows. She dances as if she *was* the music. All the movements flow from the beat. The white girls are clumsy and seem to dance against the music' (36–37). Kate, like the other white girls, cannot make her feet move 'right' (37), and wanders away. Lorena disappears from the tale having served her stereotypical purpose.

A much more extended inclusion of a Black character is from John Linklater in 'Bobby Chocolate'. Linklater tells a wry story of two white teachers looking for a Black boy who has run off from school after being called Bobby Chocolate by his peers, not for the first time. Arthur, the teacher who finds him, is 'young and inexperienced' (74) and tries to explain racism to the Black child by saying, 'There are many differences among the peoples of this world. These differences will always be there. . . . You must learn to face up to these differences. You must learn how to face up to these people who are unkind to you' (75). This echoes Rachel Scott's advice to her British Asian children in *A Wedding Man Is Nicer Than Cats*, but Linklater's story shows the child's response. The boy runs off, realising that Arthur's advice is meaningless to an everyday lived reality of racism. The other white teacher nonetheless praises him for 'having quite a way' (76) with Black children, who he calls by a racial epithet. Linklater's astute story describes 'the truth of life' in a way more aware of realities than either Joan Tate's or Ray Pope's, indicating that racism and well-meaning suggestions that people of colour tolerate white people's intolerance are two sides of the same coin. Both approaches are fed downwards from white British adults, and neither works well for Black British children.

No Life in a Voodoo Planet: Rejecting an American Vision of Black People

Although Chambers was committed to introducing a British version of YA literature, he was not entirely averse to including American books on Topliners' lists. His success with Robert Lipsyte's *The Contender* in 1969 had proved there was an audience for depictions of African-American characters; but Chambers also wanted Topliners to expand into new areas, including science fiction. In June of 1975, Chambers wrote to Martin Pick, 'As you know, interest among adolescents in SF is said by many teachers to be growing; we have been looking for some time for SF stories of Topliner length, without much success' ('Letter to Martin Pick' 19 Jun. 1975). Kaye Webb had found success publishing the work of both Robert Heinlein and Andre Norton. Both Heinlein and Norton wrote about contemporary issues in their speculative science fiction, and the idea of 'stories [that] are seated in our lives now' (*Reluctant Reader* 57) appealed to Chambers.

However, Chambers felt that most science fiction was too long and complex for his target audience. He and Nancy Chambers edited two short story collections, *World Zero Minus* (1971) and *In Time to Come* (1973) that included many popular classic science fiction writers, including Ray Bradbury, Arthur C. Clarke, and Isaac Asimov, but they did not publish any longer works by these authors. In Britain, Pan Books (which was a division of Macmillan) owned most of the paperback rights to Heinlein's novels. Andre Norton, on the other hand, had a number of different publishers, and in 1975 Chambers found one of her novels that would be new to the British public. Norton's 'Voodoo Planet has never, to the best of my knowledge, been published in this country. It was handed on to me by Joanna Goldsworthy from Gollancz, one of Norton's two publishers in this country, as a book not right for her list, but which might suit Topliners' ('Letter to Martin Pick' 19 Jun. 1975). The story had been published by Ace in the United States along with another story by Norton, but Chambers thought that by publishing *Voodoo Planet* on its own, it might be manageable for reluctant readers.

Even though Chambers felt *Voodoo Planet* 'has everything – and a terrific title, which itself will draw a number of readers' ('Letter to Martin Pick' 19 Jun. 1975), it was never included in Topliners. Despite his enthusiasm for the story, Chambers also admits in his letter to Martin Pick a certain unease about it that originated from the very aspects that excited Chambers. The book's focus on 'the actions of the story [rather] than with the finer points of character-delving' (*Reluctant Reader* 57) made it stand out for Chambers, but nonetheless he hesitated about the book, writing, 'Of course the situation of the story is that some white space men are coming to help a black and obviously "native", black man and people. Whether this is strong enough to cause bother, I'm not sure' ('Letter to Martin Pick' 19 Jun. 1975'). Chambers recognises that the white saviour narrative of Norton's book might be considered racist; however, he is still not sure it is enough 'to cause bother'. Norton's story was never published in Topliners. About this time in Topliners' publishing history, Chambers and Pick were both beginning to think about books specifically for Black and Asian readers, and perhaps they recognised that Norton's book might 'cause bother' to them even if not to white readers.

The East End Is Somewhere around Here: Courting the Black and Asian Reader

In his 1969 critical book *Reluctant Reader*, Chambers included recommended booklists for teenagers. Although several books included characters of colour (including some protagonists of colour), only one book on all of his lists is written by a Black writer: E. R. Braithwaite's *To Sir, with Love*. By the mid-1970s, Chambers felt that more representation was necessary to reach Black British and British Asian readers. He and senior editor, Martin Pick, sought out Black and Asian authors they thought might be able to write for them. As early as 1974, the editorial team at Topliners were beginning to think about what was missing from the imprint. Despite having forty-two books in print, and having sold half a million books by

1973 ('Topliners 1974 Catalogue'), Chambers was concerned that they were not reaching readers of colour (Pearson 140). They wanted writers to speak to this experience, but it took a concerted effort for white Topliners staff to locate Black and Asian writers interested in producing books for young people.

They wanted to attract Black and Asian readers as well. Pick sent one of his staff to a multiracial girls' school in Hackney to ask teachers (notably not the students directly) about their and their students' opinions on Topliners in June 1974. Teachers reported that girls preferred familiar settings, adding, 'They had not had much success among the West Indian girls with books set in the Caribbean. The girls were interested in other English girls, like themselves. They would, of course, be very interested in books about West Indians living in London' ('Internal Office Memo to Martin Pick'). Martin Wace, editorial director of Macmillan Education, was also on the lookout for suitable stories that could be reprinted for Topliners. He asked Jessica Huntley, editor of independent Black British press Bogle L'Ouverture, to send Andrew Salkey's *Joey Tyson* (1974), a fictional account of the exiling of political activist Walter Rodney, for possible republication ('Letter to Bogle L'Ouverture'). Although Huntley sent the book, it was not published in Topliners, perhaps because Chambers and Pick believed that a story set in the Caribbean, despite being 'action-packed' would not appeal to Black readers born in London.

This was certainly the case with author Michael Anthony, who had been published in New Windmill and who had been recommended by Bill Lennox, then manager of Macmillan's Caribbean lists. Early in 1975, Anthony suggested a narrative biography of artist Edwin Hingwen. Lennox passed the letter on to Chambers, who wrote back suggesting, 'On the face of it a story about a water-colour artist wouldn't immediately interest our readers' ('Letter to Michael Anthony'). However, he offered a small advance on an undetermined story that Anthony might produce by September of that year, with the caveat that they could reject the manuscript and Anthony would return the advance. Although Anthony would publish again with Macmillan Caribbean, he does not seem to have ever completed a successful Topliner – again, perhaps because, based in the Caribbean, he could not offer anything appealing for Black British readers.

With their failure to commission Caribbean writers' work for Topliners, Chambers began to look in earnest for Black British writers. Bodley Head's Judy Taylor suggested Petronella Breinburg, who had authored several picture books. Wace, who had commissioned Leila Berg to create a reading series for working-class children, may have pointed out that Breinburg had done previous work for Berg's Nippers. Late in 1975, Pick asked Peggy Costello to locate a statement written by Berg on writing for 'immigrant children' (Costello). In the 1969 statement, Berg had written, 'The majority of children . . . cannot read <u>about themselves</u>. This is what we are trying to remedy. To do this we want to find not merely people with sympathy, or even enthusiasm – quite definitely these are not enough. We want people who are familiar enough with the situation they are writing about' (Berg; underlining in original). The memo from Costello does not indicate why Pick wanted this statement, but by this time they had already contracted Breinburg, who Berg had 'discovered' through a visit to John La Rose's New Beacon bookshop, to write for Topliners. Breinburg's novel, *Us Boys of Westcroft*, appeared on the 1975 list.

Us Boys of Westcroft is the first Topliner with a Black British protagonist, and the story is narrated from Walter's first-person viewpoint. A fourteen-year-old in care, Walter has been given a chance to attend a 'posh' school. Language is a key issue in this book, and given that Breinburg herself came to England from Dutch Surinam, and spoke Dutch rather than English as her first European language, this is no surprise. Walter has to learn to speak 'posh' English so that he does not look stupid; but at the same time, he knows his own speech will often be misunderstood by white kids. 'If a white person can't understand a black, that's all right. They aren't supposed to be able to understand blacks' language, but blacks have to understand white people's language or the black is backward' (16). A language hierarchy existed between Chambers and Breinburg as well. Breinburg's original manuscript contained a far greater proportion of what Chambers called 'Surinese English' (Pearson 183), but Chambers edited most of it out to make it readable for a white reader. Although he admitted later that he had 'over-edited it' (Pearson 183), his desire to do so in the first place suggests that Chambers placed a higher value on white British English than on Black British English – much like white Britons that Breinburg's Walter describes.

Despite Chambers' editing, the book was still attacked for 'bad language' (Pearson 146), even though there was no more swearing than found in many earlier Topliners. Chambers suggested that attention to the book's language came in part from its being written by a Black author, ironically echoing Breinburg's sentiment that white people have difficulty with Black speech, and the only way to succeed is for Black people to speak like white people. However, Chambers persisted in searching for writers of colour, and the next author he championed was Indian-born schoolteacher – and former British Black Panther – Farrukh Dhondy. Dhondy came to the attention of Martin Pick who, according to Dhondy in 'The Black Writer in Britain', 'sought me out, having read my stories in the Black Panther publication *Freedom News*, to ask if he could publish them, because there was very little being written about multicultural Britain. I said I would write new ones and from this came *East End at Your Feet*' (189). Given the notoriety that *East End at Your Feet* achieved in Britain, it is perhaps a good thing that Pick did not get his wish to have Dhondy's Black Panther stories published. Dhondy's book caused almost-instant controversy, with salacious headlines in the *Daily Telegraph* and the *Daily Mail* when the white mother of a schoolgirl complained it was obscene (later, it was discovered that the mother was a member of the National Front, according to Wade in 'Novel Approach'). Chambers responded to the media in *The Bookseller*, commenting that *East End at Your Feet* was 'written by an Asian about the experiences of Asians in Britain' ('Obscenity Alleged' 2833), and that the need for such books 'had been demonstrated by the recently announced Collins prize for children's books reflecting the experience of living in multi-ethnic Britain' (2833). Chambers' defence of *East End at Your Feet* may have raised Dhondy's profile with the Collins prize, as Dhondy would go on to win it with his next book of short stories, *Come to Mecca* (1978).

Headmasters also wrote letters of complaint to Macmillan about Dhondy's language and obscenity. Michael Wace had a standard response to these letters (there are at least two nearly identical letters to complainants in the Seven Stories archives) which patiently (possibly patronisingly) explained that Dhondy's book was designed for older readers, and the much-cited passage in which a young Asian girl listens to sexually explicit Rolling Stones lyrics indicates 'the social pressures which Asian teenagers living in English cities have to face'. However, Chambers (and Wace) faced controversy within Macmillan over *East End at Your Feet* as well. In January 1977, David Fothergill, the overseas marketing director for Macmillan, noted that overseas representatives were 'meeting extreme difficulties in some countries with the "risqué content" of some titles'. Fothergill warned of a ban on the series and asked for a list of books that might cause offence. Chambers complained that Fothergill did not mention any particular titles causing the overseas representatives difficulties, but suggested that it was likely the controversy over Dhondy's book that had caused the concern ('Letter to David Fothergill').

The potentially 'risqué' titles that Chambers sent to Fothergill are worthy of examination, however. Of the five titles Chambers suggests, three of them were first published in other countries (two were by Swedish authors and one by an Australian); the other two were Breinburg's and Dhondy's. Pearson notes that foreign books allowed Chambers the opportunity to introduce 'some significantly different attitudes from those which prevailed in Britain' (160). In many ways, Breinburg's and Dhondy's books were performing similar work, introducing white Britons to significantly different attitudes – but the difference is that Dhondy and Breinburg were writing about people with different attitudes *in Britain*. Dhondy's and Breinburg's books attempted to expand the definition of Britishness, but Dhondy knew that white British people – particularly adults – would not necessarily see it that way. 'If you're a black writer writing stories for young people, you can't escape being seen by teachers and examination syllabuses as someone who will explain blacks to whites' ('The Black Writer in Britain' 190). Breinburg and Dhondy effectively acted as translators of Black and Asian experiences in Britain for white readers, but many readers – or at least their parents – did not want to admit that there was a Black British or British Asian experience, particularly when it made white Britons appear bigoted, exclusionary, or intolerant.

Chambers published one more book each by Dhondy and Breinburg. Breinburg offered several more stories, but Chambers only published *One Day, Another Day* (1977) in his Rockets series for younger readers. The book includes 'comic adventures' of two girls, one Black British and one white British, who although good-hearted often find themselves in scrapes. For Breinburg, the cross-racial friendship was important, and yet when the book was published, it included a cover with only the Black girl character on the cover – being held by a white man as if she had done something wrong. This image conforms to one white British adults often had of Black British young people, that they were criminals. As Paul Gilroy writes, the wider British population embraced 'images of a disorderly and criminal black population' (88). Chambers, despite his progressive ideas, did not object to the cover, which suggests that many ideas about Black British youth were ingrained by societal and media images.

Chambers also published Dhondy's *Siege of Babylon* (1978), a novel based on the events of the Spaghetti House Siege, in which three young black men took nine staff at the Knightsbridge Spaghetti House hostage in 1975. The book was first published in Macmillan's hardback library editions, and in Topliners only later, but it caused concern from Macmillan administrators aware of the controversy over Dhondy's *East End at Your Feet*. Alyn Shipton wrote an internal memo to Michael Wace insisting that 'in view of some of the expletives in the book, and secondly because of the nearly explicit sex scenes in it I feel that you must read it and give your approval before we do this'. The book was certainly no more explicit than some others published on the list in terms of sexual activity or language, but it was highly critical of white liberal involvement in Black civil rights activism, and it was this aspect that some white critics focused on in their reviews. The main white character, other than the police, is a young married woman named Edwina who has affairs with two of the main Black characters. Edwina runs a drama group Rupert attends; she meets him outside the group to 'talk black politics' (*East End at Your Feet* 42). Edwina finds the Black community both 'menacing . . . and exciting at the same time' (62); after her affair with Rupert she dumps him for the more dangerous Kwate, leader of the siege. In the end, however, she helps police to arrest the young Black men, describing her actions as 'a way of finishing with the world she had flirted with' (151). Dhondy depicts Edwina as a white woman using her privilege to get what Rupert defined as 'a bit of black' (75) while pretending to be interested in Black power and justice. In the end, she can simply walk away from the damage she has caused.

In 'Skin Colour in British Children's Books' Rees argues that 'one of the reasons for Dhondy's success is that, being coloured himself, he experienced and is able to present vividly some of the complexities of race relations that often escape the notice of white authors' (92). But while Rees sees this as a mark of success, many other critics do not. Rather than see Dhondy's presentation of Edwina as an indictment of ingrained white racist attitudes, Maggie Hewitt says that the book 'worries me' (25) because of its 'racist and sexist views' (25), and Rosemary Stones commented that 'Dhondy's novel *Siege of Babylon* was marred by its sexist perception of the white woman, Edwina' (23). Despite the fact that the Black body had been exoticised and eroticised by white people throughout British history, including in YA fiction I discuss in this Element, Dhondy is criticised by white people for exposing this form of racism. Nora Berenstain argues that this kind of criticism is an example of white feminist gaslighting, in which 'structural oppressions are maintained in part through systems of justification that locate the causes of pervasive inequalities in flaws of the oppressed groups themselves while obscuring the social systems and mechanisms of power that uphold them' (734). British children's and young adult literary criticism was, at the time, almost exclusively white. White feminists, such as Stones and Hewitt, by focusing only on the white female character, fail to acknowledge their own participation in racist structures.

Unlike the defence of Dhondy's *East End at Your Feet*, Chambers failed to speak up about white feminist criticism of Dhondy's work. Dhondy explained his character depictions by saying that he did not want to perpetuate the stereotype of Black British and British Asians being 'a community relations exercise' (Wade 11). 'The temptation is to show West Indians as poor, hapless and unemployed with identity crises', he argued in the same article (11). James Procter argues that white British society placed a higher 'burden of representation' (104) on writers like Dhondy, requiring them to reflect 'a more democratic, or *representative* society' (104). Dhondy depicted characters 'refusing to be spoken for by white means of mediation' (106). He believed his main audience – teenagers – could understand the portrayal of Edwina as part of the overarching difficulty for Black and Asian youth in succeeding in British society, as both white British pity and lust for the erotic appeal of the Other prevented Black and Asian youth from being seen as fully human.

Following the publication of *Siege of Babylon*, Dhondy's and Chambers' relationship soured. Dhondy clearly believed that Chambers wanted to publish progressive material for Black and Asian youth, and yet needed to be convinced to produce literature that might engender discomfort in the white establishment. Dhondy recommended another writer to Chambers: the dub poet Linton Kwesi Johnson, perhaps most famous for poems such as 'Inglan is a Bitch'. Just before the publication of *Siege*, Dhondy wrote to Martin Pick, one of Chambers' editors at Topliners: 'I've spoken to you several times about Linton Kwesi Johnson. I've tried to urge him on occasion to write some stories, produce a novel for Topliners' ('Letter to Martin Pick'). Johnson, according to Dhondy, was interested in creating a 'Reggae yearbook', something that Dhondy felt would appeal to readers but not necessarily the editors: 'I feel that Macmillan Education won't want to handle this subject at all' ('Letter to Martin Pick'). Nevertheless, he asked that Johnson's synopsis be passed on to the appropriate department. Chambers, who responds to this letter on 21 October, thanks Dhondy for 'being such a good ambassador' ('Letter to Farrukh Dhondy' 21 Oct. 1977) but does not mention Johnson or his project at all – suggesting that Dhondy's hesitation about Topliners welcoming a writer like Johnson was indeed warranted.

Dhondy's own attempts to go in a different direction also met with negativity from Topliners staff. Writing to Chambers in February of 1978, Dhondy told him that his new stories 'are work along new lines, they're not as naïve or sterilely competent as the East End ones' ('Letter to Aidan Chambers'). Although Chambers wrote back that he was 'glad you feel you're developing' ('Letter to Farrukh Dhondy', 27 Feb. 1978), the book, which was provisionally titled *Sarbatwalla Chowk*, was never published by Macmillan. Set in India, Dhondy's book was, according to Pick, 'not specifically a children's book at all ... it may in end be easiest to place this on a teenage fiction list, hoping to sell it into the adult market as well, rather than the other way round'. But Chambers, who published translated books set in Europe in Topliners to widen the experience of readers beyond Britain, was not interested in a book set in India. Communication between

Dhondy and the Topliners staff became terse, and then stopped altogether. The book, retitled *Poona Company*, would be published by Gollancz in 1980 on their adult list.

Chambers' relationship with Breinburg also ended around this time. By January 1977, *Us Boys of Westcroft* had sold over 9,000 copies, exceeding most Topliner sales. Breinburg, perhaps hoping to capitalise on this success, offered Chambers a similarly titled but non-fiction manuscript, *Sex and Us Girls*. She wrote, pointing out her success in girls' schools and prodding him about the manuscript, saying she did not expect to hear from him right away 'because you may have to consult head office' ('Letter to Aidan Chambers'). Chambers wrote back, apologising that 'there is nowhere on the Topliner list we could publish it as it isn't at all the sort of thing we are doing at the moment' ('Letter to Petronella Breinburg'). It is difficult to know what Chambers meant by this; certainly, the imprint had started to move into non-fiction, with books on scrambling, fishing, and popular music due out in March 1977 and planned books on poetry and folktales. And Chambers was clearly not squeamish about sex in books for teenagers. But this book, and several others that Breinburg followed it with, were never quite right for Topliners. Breinburg, like Dhondy, continued to have success in publishing, but never again with Topliners or Macmillan.

In fact, Chambers never again published another Topliner by a Black British or British Asian writer. The imprint continued in some form until the 1980s, but Chambers gave up his post as general editor in 1979. He felt that books for young people, which had once been controlled by people (like Peacock editor Kaye Webb, perhaps) who demanded a certain level of literariness, 'was quickly shifting to the judgement of groups of adults … who always claimed to be working on behalf of children's own opinions and "rights"' ('Axes for Frozen Seas' 14). This group of adults surely included Rosemary Stones and Andrew Mann, who set up the Children's Rights Workshop and the Other Award, and Robert Leeson, who wrote about political aspects of children's literature including racism and sexism. Stones and Leeson had publicly championed Chambers' work with Topliners, and *East End at Your Feet* had won the Other Award in 1976, but both critics felt that it was important that books for young people demonstrate clearly anti-racist *and* anti-sexist principles in an uncomplicated way. This often meant creating one-dimensional characters, something Dhondy would not do. Dhondy and Chambers both objected to the notion that there was only one way to portray Blackness or Asianness, but Dhondy's portrayals were designed for Black British and British Asian readers, and Chambers had to be concerned about white British readers as well. Rather than engage with the debate about what constituted 'good' anti-racist literature, Chambers stepped away from his editorial and publishing role altogether.

Despite Chambers' desire to expand the type of book available to readers, and to promote Black British and British Asian authors, he was ultimately more interested in an idea of literary quality associated with white British literature and with the 'universal' character of the teenager than he was with anti-racism. His editing and re-editing of Petronella Breinburg's work, his disinterest in material set in the Caribbean or India (despite being eager to translate work from Europe), and his hostility towards children's rights advocates result in a paucity of YA literature by and for Black British and British Asian readers on the Topliners list. Chambers may have had a more egalitarian vision than either Webb or Serraillier, but the literature he produced in Topliners only gave the smallest glimpse of how it was 'always like this' for the Black and Asian teenager living in Britain.

Conclusion: A Positive Approach from Society towards Integration? British Young Adult Literature and White Privilege

In Ian Serraillier's reader report about Rachel Scott's *A Wedding Man Is Nicer Than Cats, Miss*, he compares the book favourably to E. R. Braithwaite's *To Sir, with Love*:

> The nearest approach to this book that we have in the series is 'To Sir, With Love'. Though Rachel Scott's book has not the advantage of a film to back its appeal, it seems to us the better of the two books. It is not so much concerned with the teacher and his own excellence as with a positive approach from society towards integration.
>
> ('Readers Report *Wedding Man*')

Both books focus on a teacher's experience of the interactions of a multiracial school and the way that they were received by their students. Yet Braithwaite is portrayed as being concerned with his own excellence while Scott is providing a positive approach to integration. Braithwaite, as I discussed earlier, does not try to make white readers comfortable. He describes his near-daily experiences of racism, and those of his students, both big and small. Scott, on the contrary, not only tries to make white readers comfortable in this 'new situation to which we have previously not been accustomed' (11) – an 'advent of a significant number of coloured immigration, and their accumulation in large cities' (11 – she also tries to make herself, the white teacher, comfortable. Scott gives historical reasons for her Asian students' 'deep dislike' (190) of West Indians, considering this a failing on their part, but describes shuddering at niqabs and telling students not to follow the cultural traditions of their home country as part of her own success. Serraillier's opinion that Scott wrote the better book underscores the idea that Black and Brown people should accept white Britons' ideas of Britishness.

This is not to say that Serraillier – or indeed, Webb or Chambers – deliberately set out to further a white supremacist agenda in publishing and editing literature for young adults. Quite the contrary, all these editors made attempts to reach out to readers in Black and Asian British communities. But those attempts were, like Rachel Scott's teaching, often focused on an impossible goal: embracing Black British and British Asian stories while at the same time suggesting integration as the only means of success in society. The impossibility was rooted in the fact that YA literature, invented as a response to fears about the teenager after the war, participated in what Nicole Jackson calls 'the nationalist project that emerged after the World War II which replaced an imperial (British) identity with a national (English) identity, understood as exclusively White' ('The Ties That Bind' 118). Mainstream and educational publishing participated in this project because books for young people, as Sheila Ray commented, 'must meet the standards demanded by the institutional market of public libraries and schools' (195); and libraries and schools were bound up in ideas about citizenship and Britishness.

Paul Gilroy comments that 'the absolutist view of black and white cultures, as fixed, mutually impermeable expressions of racial and national identity, is a ubiquitous theme in racial "common sense", but it is far from secure' (68). British Black Panther and civil rights activist Darcus Howe argued in 1974 that white 'institutions of liberalism [act] as prime agents of social control' (11) and that this attempt at control would lead to 'black revolt' (12) in the form of 'independent grass-roots self-activity with a view to furthering its development' (12). Between 1960 and 1980, white mainstream British publishing largely ignored, stereotyped, or attempted to integrate Black British and British Asian readers. When, like Webb's attempt to take the Puffin Club to Lambeth, these efforts failed to produce enthusiastic Black and Asian British readers, editors labelled them 'non-readers'. But Black and Asian Britons were not non-readers; they just looked elsewhere for their reading material. Rob Waters, in *Thinking Black*, suggests that many young Black and Asian Britons turned 'to the literature of American civil rights and Black Power' (56). They bought and read this material, not in high-street shops, mainstream education, or public libraries, but in Black- and Asian-run grassroots establishments. Waters continues, 'Confronting this difficulty of accessing black literature, community activists established black resource centres as radical alternatives to public libraries' (59). The poet Linton Kwesi Johnson was one beneficiary of alternative libraries provided by Black organisations: 'It was in the [Black] Panthers that I discovered literature, Black literature, because we were encouraged to read' (154). He goes on to discuss the profound effect reading books such as W. E. B. DuBois' *The Souls of Black Folk* had, writing, "I wanted to read more and to write and to express my own ideas and my own feelings and my experiences growing up in England' (155). And where white librarians wondered about the rights and wrongs of piping in popular music or allowing young adults to dance and drink coffee in public libraries, Black and Asian communities welcomed the breaking of the book's boundaries. Dub poetry, by Black poets such as Johnson, could be listened to on records (*Dread Beat and Blood* was produced by Front Line Records in 1978) or read in books (the collection of poems was published by independent Black British publisher Bogle L'Ouverture) – but not in books published by Webb, Serraillier, and Chambers. John La Rose, the founder of independent Black publishing house New Beacon Press, argued that Black publishers 'did everything oneself and developed networks ... to the extent where the basis of self-reliance was firmly rooted' (Lloyd 38). This meant that much of the material written for and by people of colour was published by smaller, independent firms that appreciated and nurtured their authors but did not have the (inter)national reach of Penguin, Macmillan, or Heinemann.

The legacy of years of white, middle-class domination of British YA literature continues today. Melanie Ramdarshan Bold, in her book *Inclusive Young Adult Fiction*, comments that even now, 'many authors of colour felt pressure to write identity books' (33), and yet 'such books often had to adhere to Western interpretations of nationality and/or ethnicity' (33). And while efforts to 'do everything oneself', as John La Rose suggested, also still continue, they are not enough. Reni Eddo-Lodge says, 'We need to change narratives. ... We need to claim the entirety of British history. We need to let it be known that black is British, that brown is British, and that we are not going away' (223). Eddo-Lodge's 'we' is Black and Brown Britons, not white Britons, but until mainstream publishing (if ever) is no longer dominated by white editors and publishers, and until all children experience being taught and guided into books by people of colour, white Britons involved in YA literature must be involved in change as well. Black British and British Asian YA literature is British literature, and all readers – no matter what their background – need to be able to see, understand, and enjoy their stories in order to fully understand and participate in the nation in which they live.

References

Abrams, Mark. 'The £900 m. Teenage Market'. *Financial Times*, 11 Feb. 1959, p. 6.

'At the Peacock Think-In'. *Puffin Post*, vol. 5, no. 3, 1971, p. 29.

'Author of *Walkabout* Who Preferred Anonymity'. *Sydney Morning Herald*, 12 Oct. 2018,www.smh.com.au/national/author-of-walkabout-who-preferred-anonymity-20181009-p508lv.html. Accessed 13 Dec. 2020.

Baecker, Dianne L. 'Surviving Rescue: A Feminist Reading of Scott O'Dell's *Island of the Blue Dolphins*'. *Children's Literature in Education*, vol. 38, 2007, pp. 195–206.

Banfield, Beryle. 'Commitment to Change: The Council on Interracial Books for Children and the World of Children's Books'. *African American Review*, vol. 32, no. 1, 1998, pp. 17–22.

Bawden, Nina. *On the Run*. 1964. New Windmill, 1967.

Beal, Tony. 'Ian Serraillier'. *Guardian*, 6 Dec. 1994, A17.

Belaney, Archibald [Grey Owl]. *Sajo and her Beaver People*. 1935. New Windmill, 1967.

Berenstain, Nora. 'White Feminist Gaslighting'. *Hypatia*, vol. 35, 2020, pp. 733–58.

Berg, Leila. 'February 1969'. Uncatalogued memo, Aidan Chambers Archive, Seven Stories National Centre for Children's Books.

'Big "Teenage" Spending'. *Sunday Times*, 8 Mar. 1959, p. 8.

Birley, Hilary. 'Letter to D. M. Marsh'. 6 Apr. 1967. Heinemann Educational Books Publishers Archive, University of Reading. HEB NW 2/18.

Bold, Melanie Ramdarshan. *Inclusive Young Adult Fiction: Authors of Colour in the United Kingdom*. Palgrave Pivot, 2019.

Braithwaite, E. R. *To Sir, with Love*. 1959. New Windmill, 1971.

Breinburg, Petronella. 'Letter to Aidan Chambers'. 15 Jan. 1977. Seven Stories National Centre for Children's Books Archives.

One Day, Another Day. Macmillan Rockets, 1977.

Us Boys of Westcroft. Macmillan Topliners, 1975.

Breyley, Gay. 'Fearing the Protector, Fearing the Protected: Indigenous and "National" Fears in Twentieth-Century Australia'. *Antipodes*, vol. 23, no. 1, Jun. 2009, pp.43–8.

Buchan, John. *The Three Hostages*. 1924. Peacock, 1963.

Chambers, Aidan. 'Axes for Frozen Seas'. *Booktalk: Occasional Writing on Literature and Children*. Thimble Press, 1995, pp. 14–33.

'Letter from England: American Writing and British Readers'. *Booktalk: Occasional Writing on Literature and Children*. Thimble Press, 1995, pp. 77–83.

'Letter to David Fothergill'. 25 Jan. 1977. Seven Stories National Centre for Children's Books Archives.

'Letter to Farrukh Dhondy'. 27 Feb. 1978. Seven Stories National Centre for Children's Books Archives.

'Letter to Farrukh Dhondy'. 21 Oct. 1977. Seven Stories National Centre for Children's Books Archives.

'Letter to Martin Pick'. 4 May 1975. Seven Stories National Centre for Children's Books Archives.

'Letter to Martin Pick'. 19 Jun. 1975. Seven Stories National Centre for Children's Books Archives.

'Letter to Michael Anthony'. 22 Feb. 1975. Seven Stories National Centre for Children's Books Archives.

'Letter to Petronella Breinburg'. 31 Jan. 1977. Seven Stories National Centre for Children's Books Archives.

'Proposal for a TOPLINERS Magazine'. 9 Mar. 1973. Seven Stories National Centre for Children's Books Archives.

The Reluctant Reader. Pergamon, 1969.

'Topliners Press Release'. 18 Sept. 1975. Aidan Chambers Archive, Seven Stories National Centre for Children's Books.

Chambers, Aidan (ed.). *I Want to Get Out*. Topliners, 1971.

'Church Urges Need for Sex Education'. *Daily Telegraph*, 28 Oct. 1950, p. 5.

Coard, Bernard. *How the West Indian Is Made Educationally Sub Normal in the British School System: The Scandal of the Black Child in Schools in Britain*. New Beacon, 1971.

Cohen, Philip. 'The Perversions of Inheritance: Studies in the Making of Multi-Racist Britain'. *Multi-Racist Britain*. Eds. Philip Cohen and Harwant S. Bains. Macmillan, 1988, pp.9–18.

Corbett, Jim. *Man-Eaters of Kumaon*. 1944. Peacock, 1964.

Costello, Peggy. 'Internal Office Memo'. 7 Oct. 1975. Aidan Chambers Archive, Seven Stories National Centre for Children's Books.

Darke, Marjorie. *The First of Midnight*. Peacock, 1979.

Dhondy, Farrukh. 'The Black Writer in Britain'. *Here to Stay, Here to Fight: A Race Today Anthology*. Eds. Paul Field, Robin Bunce, Leila Hassan, and Margaret Peacock. Pluto, 2019, pp. 185–91.

  Come to Mecca. Collins Cascades, 1978.

  East End at Your Feet. Macmillan Topliners, 1976.

  'Letter to Aidan Chambers'. 20 Feb. 1978. Aidan Chambers Archive, Seven Stories National Centre for Children's Books.

  'Letter to Martin Pick'. 15 Oct. 1977. Aidan Chambers Archive, Seven Stories National Centre for Children's Books.

  Siege of Babylon. Macmillan, 1978.

Diangelo, Robin. *White Fragility: Why It's So Hard for White People to Talk about Racism*. Allen Lane, 2019.

'Did Grey Owl "Spoof" Hull Public?' *Hull Daily Mail*, 20 Apr. 1938, p. 1.

Dunphy, Eamon. 'Millwall vs. the Mob'. *The Millwall History Files*, www .millwall-history.org.uk. Accessed 13 Dec. 2020.

  Only a Game? The Diary of a Professional Footballer. 1976. Peacock, 1977.

Eddo-Lodge, Reni. *Why I'm No Longer Talking to White People about Race*. Bloomsbury, 2018.

Fenwick, I. G. K. *The Comprehensive School 1944–1970*. Methuen, 1976.

'Fiction of Their Time'. *Guardian*, 22 Apr. 1986, p. 14.

Fothergill, David. 'Letter to Aidan Chambers'. 17 Jan. 1977. Aidan Chambers Archive, Seven Stories National Centre for Children's Books.

Fryer, Peter. *Staying Power: The History of Black People in Britain*. New edition. Pluto, 2018.

'Gang Attacks Police'. *Daily Mail*, 29 Jun. 1959, p. 7.

Gárdonyi, Géza. *Slave of the Huns*. Peacock, 1973.

Garstin, Crosbie. *The Owls' House*. Peacock, 1964.

Gerzina, Gretchen Holbrook. *Black London: Life before Emancipation*. Rutgers University Press, 1995.

Gillard, Derek. *Education in England: A History*, 2018, www.educationeng land.org.uk/history. Accessed 13 Dec. 2020.

Gilroy, Paul. *There Ain't No Black in the Union Jack*. 1987. Routledge, 1992.

Glaskin, G. M. *A Waltz through the Hills*. 1961. New Windmill, 1964.
A Waltz through the Hills. Rev. ed. Peacock, 1970.

Godden, Rumer. *The Peacock Spring*. 1975. Peacock, 1977.

Goldberg, Carole. 'A Counterstory of Native American Persistence'. *Island of the Blue Dolphins: Complete Reader's Edition*, pp. 219–28.

Graham, Eleanor. 'The Puffin Years'. *Signal*, vol. 12, Sept. 1973, pp.115–22.

Griffiths, Susan C. '"So the Very Young Know and Understand": Reframing Discussion of *The Cay*'. *Horn Book*, vol. 88, no. 5, pp. 27–31.

Grove, Valerie. 'Kaye Webb'. *Puffins Progress*. Penguin Collectors Society, 2014, pp.49–66.

Hall, Catherine. *Civilising Subjects*. Polity, 2002.

Hall, John. 'Parents Warned: Bad Boys Are Your Fault'. *Daily Mail*, 1 Jun. 1951, p. 2.

Hannabuss, Stuart. 'What We Used to Read: A Survey of Children's Reading in Britain, 1910–1950'. *Children's Literature in Education*, vol. 8, no. 3, autumn 1977, pp. 127–34.

'Hard for Youth to Grow Up'. *The Times*, 7 Jan. 1955, p. 5.

Hare, Steve. *Penguin Portrait: Allen Lane and the Penguin Editors, 1935–1970*. Penguin, 1995.

Heinlein, Robert A. *Citizen of the Galaxy*. 1957. Peacock, 1972.

Hewitt, Maggie. 'Review: The Siege of Babylon'. *Children's Book Bulletin*, no. 2, autumn 1979, p. 25.

Hill, Janet. *Children Are People: The Librarian in the Community*. Hamish Hamilton, 1973.

Howe, Darcus. 'From Victim to Protagonist: The Changing Social Reality'. *Here to Stay, Here to Fight: A Race Today Anthology*. Eds. Paul Field, Robin Bunce, Leila Hassan, and Margaret Peacock. Pluto, 2019, pp. 10–12.

Iddon, Don. 'Rock 'n Roll Is Musical Dynamite'. *Daily Mail*, 4 Sept. 1956, p. 4.

Ifekwunigwe, Jayne O. 'Re-Membering "Race": On Gender, "Mixed Race" and Family in the English-African Diaspora'. *Rethinking 'Mixed Race'*. Eds. David Parker and Miri Song. Pluto, 2001, pp. 42–64.

'Internal Office Memo to Martin Pick'. 17 Jun. 1974, Aidan Chambers Archive, Seven Stories National Centre for Children's Books.

Jackson, Nicole M. 'The Ties That Bind: Questions of Empire and Belonging in Black British Educational Activism'. *Blackness in Britain*. Eds. Kehinde Andrews and Lisa Amanda Palmer. Routledge, 2016, pp. 117–29.

Johnson, Linton Kwesi. 'The Problem of the Colour Line'. *Tell It Like It Is: How Our Schools Fail Black Children*. Ed. Brian Richardson. Bookmarks, 2005, pp. 153–5.

Jones, Linda Lloyd. 'Fifty Years of Penguin Books'. *Fifty Penguin Years*. [no editor listed] Penguin, 1985, pp. 11–103.

Kamm, Josephine. *Out of Step*. 1962. New Windmill, 1969.

Kata, Elizabeth. *A Patch of Blue*. 1961. Peacock, 1977.

Kaufmann, Miranda. *Black Tudors: The Untold Story*. Oneworld, 2017.

Kendrick, Faith. 'Lunchbreak'. *I Want to Get Out*. Ed. Aidan Chambers. Macmillan, 1971, pp. 35–8.

Knight, Christine. 'Teenage Library at Lincoln'. *Library World*, vol. 71, no. 833, Nov. 1969, pp. 40–6.

Lewis, Naomi. *The Best Children's Books of 1964*. Hamish Hamilton, 1965.

Linklater, John. 'Bobby Chocolate'. *I Want to Get Out*. Ed. Aidan Chambers. Macmillan, 1971, pp. 73–6.

Lipsyte, Robert. *The Contender*. Macmillan Topliners, 1969.

Lloyd, Errol. 'The International Book Fair of Radical Black and Third World Books: An Interview with John La Rose'. *New Beacon Review*, vol. 1, Jul. 1985, pp. 27–41.

MacCann, Donnarae. *White Supremacy in Children's Literature*. Taylor and Francis, 2000.

MacKenzie, John. *Propaganda and Empire: The Manipulation of British Opinion 1880–1960*. Manchester University Press, 1984.

Marshall, James Vance. *Walkabout*. 1959. Peacock, 1963.

Marshall, Margaret. *Libraries and Literature for Teenagers*. Andre Deutsch, 1975.

Martin, David. 'Unfair to Teenagers'. *Daily Mail*, 16 Jun. 1959, p. 6.

'Millwall 1977'. *Panorama*, 14 Nov. 1977. BBC television.

Moss, Elaine. 'Reluctant at Fifteen'. *The Times*, 16 Mar. 1968, p. 23.

'Need to Wean Children from Comics to Books'. *The Press* [Christchurch, New Zealand], 21 Mar. 1964, p. 2.

'Obscenity Alleged in Macmillan Book'. *Bookseller*, 25 Dec. 1976–1 Jan. 1977, p. 2833.

Olusoga, David. *Black and British: A Forgotten History*. Macmillan, 2016.

Owen, Charlie. '"Mixed Race" in Official Statistics'. *Rethinking 'Mixed Race'*. Eds. David Parker and Miri Song. Pluto, 2001, pp. 134–53.

Patterson, Sheila. *Dark Strangers: A Study of West Indians in London.* Pelican, 1965.

'Peacock Questionnaire'. *Puffin Post*, vol. 5, no. 2, 1971, p. 1.

'Peacock Think-In'. *Puffin Post*, vol. 5, no. 3, 1971, p. 1.

Pearson, Lucy. *The Making of Modern Children's Literature in Britain: Publishing and Criticism in the 1960s and 1970s.* Ashgate, 2013.

Pearson, Lucy, Karen Sands-O'Connor, and Aishwarya Subramanian. 'Prize Culture and Diversity in British Children's Literature'. *International Research in Children's Literature*, vol. 12, no. 1, Jul. 2019, pp. 90–106.

Philpott, Trevor. 'The Truth About Teenagers'. *Picture Post*, vol. 74, no. 11, 18 Mar. 1957, pp.10–13.

Pick, Martin. 'Letter to Anne McDermid'. 13 Jul. 1979. Seven Stories National Centre for Children's Books Archives.

Pocock, Tom. 'Focus on Teenagers'. *Daily Mail*, 27 Apr. 1950, p. 4.

Pope, Ray. *Is It Always Like This?* Macmillan Topliners, 1970.

Prebble, John. *The Buffalo Soldiers*. 1959. New Windmill, 1965.

Procter, James. 'New Ethnicities, the Novel and the Burdens of Representation'. *A Concise Companion to Contemporary British Fiction*, vol. 21, no. 1, 2005, pp. 101–20.

Ray, Sheila. *Children's Fiction: A Handbook for Librarians*. Rev. Ed. Brockhampton, 1972.

Ray, Colin and Sheila (eds.). *Reader's Guide to Books on Attitudes and Adventures*. 3rd ed. Library Association, 1971.

'The Red Man Is Happy Again'. *Hull Daily Mail*, 8 Jan. 1936, p. 5.

Rees, David. 'Skin Colour in British Children's Books'. *Children's Literature in Education*, vol. 11, 1980, pp. 91–7.

Reynolds, Kimberley. *Left Out: The Forgotten Tradition of Radical Publishing for Children in Britain 1910–1949.* Oxford University Press, 2016.

Ridley, Ian. 'Marriage of Two Troubled Minds'. *Guardian*, 25 Aug. 2002, www.theguardian.com/football/2002/aug/25/sport.footballinire land. Accessed 3 Aug. 2022.

Rose, E. J. B. *Colour and Citizenship: A Report on British Race Relations*. Institute of Race Relations/Oxford University Press, 1969.

Rouleau, Brian. *Empire's Nursery: Children's Literature and the Origin of the American Century*. New York University Press, 2021.

Said, Edward. *Orientalism*. Vintage, 1979.

Sands-O'Connor, Karen. *Children's Publishing and Black Britain 1965–2015*. Palgrave Macmillan, 2017.

Soon Come Home to This Island: West Indians in British Children's Literature. Routledge, 2007.

Schwartz, Albert V. '*The Cay*: Racism Rewarded'. *Racism and Sexism in Children's Books*. Writers and Readers, pp. 45–8.

Scott, Rachel. *A Wedding Man Is Nicer Than Cats, Miss*. 1971. New Windmills, 1974.

Serraillier, Ian. 'Notes and Corrections 11 Jan. 1964'. Heinemann Educational Books Publishers Archive, University of Reading. HEB NW 2/8.

'Readers Report *Wedding Man*'. 16 Jun. 1972. Heinemann Educational Books Publishers Archive, University of Reading. HEB NW 7/7.

Serraillier, Anne. 'Letter to Hilary Birley'. 29 Jan. 1967. Heinemann Educational Books Publishers Archive, University of Reading. HEB NW 7/13.

'Letter to Tony Beal'. 30 Jun. 1969. Heinemann Educational Books Publishers Archive, University of Reading. HEB NW 11/18.

Sheahan-Bright, Robin. 'Red, Yellow, and Black: Australian Indigenous Publishing for Young People'. *Bookbird*, vol. 3, 2011, pp.1–17.

Shipton, Alyn. 'Internal Memo to Michael Wace'. 16 Dec. 1977. Aidan Chambers Archive, Seven Stories National Centre for Children's Books.

Sperry, Armstrong. *The Boy Who Was Afraid*. 1942. New Windmill, 1952.

'Newbery Acceptance Speech'. Armstrong Sperry (website). Ed. Margo Burns, 2009, http://armstrongsperry.com/papers/NewberyAcceptance.shtml.

St John, John. *William Heinemann: A Century of Publishing 1890–1990*. Heinemann, 1990.

Stones, Rosemary. 'Review: *Come to Mecca*'. *Children's Book Bulletin*, no. 1, Jun. 1979, p. 23.

'Story Competition – Older Runners-Up'. *Times Educational Supplement*, 22 May 1970, p. 14.

Sussex, Lucy. 'Review: In Search of Bony'. *Clue*, vol. 26, no. 2, winter 2008, pp. 97–9.

Tate, Joan. *Clipper*. Macmillan Topliners, 1969.

Jenny. Illus. Charles Keeping. Heinemann Joan Tate Books, 1964.

Mrs Jenny. Illus. Charles Keeping. Heinemann Joan Tate Books, 1966.

Out of the Sun. Heinemann Pyramid, 1968.

Taylor, Becky. 'Good Citizens? Ugandan Asians, Volunteers, and 'Race' Relations'. *History Workshop Journal*, vol. 85, 2018, pp. 120–41.

'Teenage Danger'. *Daily Mail*, 14 Oct. 1959, p. 5.

Thompson, Laurie, and Cleodie Mackinnon. 'Joan Tate'. *Guardian*, 7 Jul. 2000, p. 24.

Tomlinson, Norman. 'Reading for Children and Teenagers'. *Library Review*, vol. 19, no. 2, Feb. 1963, pp.98–103.

Topliners 1974 Catalogue. Aidan Chambers Archive, Seven Stories National Centre for Children's Books.

Trotman, Felicity. 'Remembering Peacock'. *Puffins Progress*. Penguin Collectors Society, 2014, pp. 71–9.

Tucker, Nicholas. 'Nina Bawden'. *Independent*, 24 Aug. 2012, www.independent.co.uk/news/obituaries/nina-bawden-author-who-drew-deeply-on-her-own-experience-in-her-novels-for-adults-and-children-8076913.html. Accessed 3 Aug. 2022.

Upfield, Arthur. *Bony and the Mouse*. 1959. New Windmill, 1961.

Wace, Michael. 'Letter to A. Walker'. 31 Dec. 1976. Aidan Chambers Archive, Seven Stories National Centre for Children's Books.

'Letter to Bogle L'Ouverture'. 18 Feb. 1975, Aidan Chambers Archive, Seven Stories National Centre for Children's Books.

Wade, Graham. 'Novel Approach'. *Guardian*, 22 Aug. 1978, p. 11.

Walden, Daniel. 'Review: *Spirit of Australia*'. *Journal of Popular Culture*, vol. 23, no. 2, autumn 1989, pp. 172–4.

Wassil, Gregory. 'Keats's Orientalism'. *Studies in Romanticism*, vol. 39, no. 3, autumn 2000, pp. 419–47.

Waters, Rob. *Thinking Black: Britain, 1964–1985*. University of California Press, 2019.

Webb, Kaye. 'Peacock Competition: Design a Cover'. *Puffin Post*, vol. 4, no. 4, 1970, p. 24.

'Kaye Webb Puffin Notes in Diary Form'. n.d. ca. 1962, Kaye Webb Archive, Seven Stories National Centre for Children's Books.

'Tony Godwin: Summary of Conversation'. Meeting notes, n.d., ca. Mar. 1961, Kaye Webb Archive, Seven Stories National Centre for Children's Books.

'What Teenagers Buy'. *Guardian*, 26 Jan. 1961, p. 12.

Williams, James H. *Elephant Bill*. 1950. Peacock, 1963.

Wilson, Des. *So You Want to Be Prime Minister? An Introduction to British Politics Today*. Peacock, 1979.

Wright, Kate. 'The Development of Puffin Books'. *Bookbird*, vol. 47, no. 1, 2009, pp. 40–5.

Yates, Jessica. 'Censorship in Children's Paperbacks'. *Children's Literature in Education*, vol. 11, 1980, pp. 180–91.

Acknowledgements

This book would not have been possible without the aid of several individuals and organisations. Most notably, the British Academy provided grant funding for my professorship at Newcastle University; Seven Stories, the United Kingdom's National Centre for Children's Books provided me with access to archival material during lockdown; and Paula Wride lent me a quiet place to work when my small flat's walls were closing in. The Special Collections at the University of Reading and series editor Melanie Ramdarshan Bold, for whom I wrote this book, also deserve many, many thanks.

Cambridge Elements ☰

Publishing and Book Culture

SERIES EDITOR

Samantha Rayner
University College London

Samantha Rayner is Professor of Publishing and Book Cultures at UCL. She is also Director of UCL's Centre for Publishing, co-Director of the Bloomsbury CHAPTER (Communication History, Authorship, Publishing, Textual Editing and Reading) and co-Chair of the Bookselling Research Network.

ASSOCIATE EDITOR

Leah Tether
University of Bristol

Leah Tether is Professor of Medieval Literature and Publishing at the University of Bristol. With an academic background in medieval French and English literature and a professional background in trade publishing, Leah has combined her expertise and developed an international research profile in book and publishing history from manuscript to digital.

About the Series

This series aims to fill the demand for easily accessible, quality texts available for teaching and research in the diverse and dynamic fields of Publishing and Book Culture. Rigorously researched and peer-reviewed Elements will be published under themes, or 'Gatherings'. These Elements should be the first check point for researchers or students working on that area of publishing and book trade history and practice: we hope that, situated so logically at Cambridge University Press, where academic publishing in the UK began, it will develop to create an unrivalled space where these histories and practices can be investigated and preserved.

Cambridge Elements ☰

Publishing and Book Culture
Young Adult Publishing

Gathering Editor: Melanie Ramdarshan Bold

Melanie Ramdarshan Bold is Senior Lecturer in Children's Literature and Literacies in the School of Education at the University of Glasgow, where she teaches and researches topics related to Children's and Young Adult literature and book culture. Her main research interest centres on developments in authorship, publishing, and reading, and inclusiveness and representation in literary culture, with a focus on books for children and young adults.

Elements in the Gathering

A full series listing is available at: www.cambridge.org/EPBC

Printed in the United States
by Baker & Taylor Publisher Services